Liberty and Civilization

Liberty
and
Civilization
The Western Heritage

edited by Roger Scruton

A Collection of Essays from
The American Spectator

Encounter Books ℯ New York · London

First American edition published in 2010 by Encounter Books,
an activity of Encounter for Culture and Education, Inc.,
a nonprofit, tax-exempt corporation.
Encounter Books website address: www.encounterbooks.com

Manufactured in the United States and printed on
acid-free paper. The paper used in this publication meets
the minimum requirements of ANSI/NISO Z39.48-1992
(R 1997) (*Permanence of Paper*).

FIRST AMERICAN EDITION

LIBRARY OF CONGRESS CATALOGING-IN-PUBLICATION DATA

Liberty and civilization : the western heritage / edited by Roger Scruton.
p. cm.
"A Collection of Essays from the American Spectator."
Includes bibliographical references and index.
ISBN-13: 978-1-59403-383-4 (hardcover : alk. paper)
ISBN-10: 1-59403-383-8 (hardcover : alk. paper) 1. Liberty. 2. Civilization,
Western. I. Scruton, Roger. II. American spectator.
JC585.L422 2010
320.01'1—dc22
2009036436

10 9 8 7 6 5 4 3 2 1

Contents

Preface

The essays in this volume originally appeared during the course of 2008 in *The American Spectator* and were commissioned with the help of a generous grant from the John Templeton Foundation, for which I and the editorial team at the *Spectator* are extremely grateful. In recent years the Templeton Foundation has played a large part in supporting the intellectual and spiritual legacy of our civilization and encouraging people to think creatively and independently about the larger questions that concern modern societies. One of these questions addresses the place of liberty in the Western heritage. As many of the essays make clear, it is not a question that can be detached from the Judaeo-Christian tradition of social thinking; and we who are heirs to that tradition are under a special obligation today, confronted by militant atheism at home and militant Islam abroad, to clarify the nature and extent of our debt to the Jewish and Christian sources. As several authors argue, without the Biblical idea of free choice as the essence of the human condition, the political systems with which we are familiar in the Western world would not have emerged.

The belief in individual liberty as the goal of political order has taken root in Europe and its diaspora largely because individual liberty has been seen as a prerequisite of the relationship between man and God. And during the Enlightenment that religious idea was given a secular elaboration, in the theory of human rights and the idea of popular sovereignty. Since then it has been widely assumed in the West that political order exists for the sake of the individual, not the other way round. It is on that assumption that our political institutions have been built, reformed, and defended. But is the assumption still valid today? And can it remain in place in a world that increasingly turns its back on the Judaeo-Christian view of the individual as the creation of a loving God, endowed with free will and personality, and fulfilled through the exercise of sovereign choice?

Those questions are now of the first importance, and this timely book of essays will surely help to clarify the thinking of those who recognize the importance of liberty in defining the political contests, both national and international, in which we in the West are now embroiled. The authors are (for the most part) of a conservative persuasion—individual liberty having become, in the face of the expanding state and the leftist assault on civil society, central to the conservative outlook. But the essays show a commendable freedom from dogmatism and an openness to argument that will, I hope, appeal to a wide audience, and in particular to those who view with concern the steady loss of liberties in Western societies today.

Rather than surveying the essays in this preface I conclude the book with an essay of my own, attempting to bring together the many themes explored by the other authors and drawing some conclusions pertinent to the great choices that we in the West now confront.

Roger Scruton
Sperryville, Virginia
December 2008

Religious Freedom and the American Inheritance

Seamus Hasson

It is fitting to begin this book with religious freedom, as defined by the First Amendment to the U.S. Constitution. For the freedom of conscience, so long taken for granted in our societies, is no longer a reality, with radical Islam extending its censorship in Europe and radical atheism attempting the same in America. Seamus Hasson, director of the Becket Fund for Religious Liberty, here considers the chequered history of religious freedom in America and the current controversies over the "no establishment" clause.

There is, perhaps, no other area of American life in which we claim to be so thoroughly united. And there is almost certainly no other area in American life in which we are, in fact, so vexingly divided.

THE MYTH

Ask nearly anyone if there is religious liberty in America and you'll get some version of The Myth: The Pilgrims came from England in search of religious freedom. They found it in Plymouth Colony, took a break for Thanksgiving Dinner, then somebody passed the First

1

Amendment and we all lived happily ever after. Push back ever so slightly and the cognitive dissonance will begin. The culture war? Yes, well, we all would be living happily ever after if it weren't for the crazies who just don't get it and are trying to shove—pick either (a) "separation of church and state" or (b) "their religion"—down our throats.

Ask either set of "crazies" whether it's really true that they oppose religious liberty? More dissonance. Nobody will ever admit to opposing religious freedom for all. On the contrary, everyone will steadfastly insist they absolutely love the stuff—which is why they are so nobly defending it against the unscrupulous fanatics on the other side.

Pose the big questions, extreme dissonance. Where does religious liberty come from? Why, it's a natural right that the First Amendment gives us. And just what does it protect? Social harmony, by allowing—pick either (a) "only the true religion" or (b) "no religion whatsoever"—to be expressed in public culture.

In short, as a society, we're at wit's end. We assume we must understand something so basic to our heritage as religious freedom. But when we actually take a look at it, all the philosophical and legal lines seem to blur and to overlap one another. Let's face it: when it comes to religious liberty, we really don't know what we think.

That is a very precarious position to be in. The cognitive dissonance might be vaguely laughable if these questions weren't so urgent. But our growing religious diversity makes them not just urgent, but fundamental to our identity. If we were living in the Vatican City State, or perhaps in a remote mountain village in Utah, we would likely not find ourselves having to debate the origins and meaning of religious freedom. The fact is, however, we are living in the most religiously diverse society in the history of the world. It is becoming more diverse by the day. And some of our new neighbors seem deadly serious—literally—about their beliefs. Now more than ever, it is essential that we know what we think about religious liberty.

A quick tour of our history will reveal the sources of our present confusion. It will demonstrate that The Myth is, well, a myth. There has never been a golden age of religious tranquillity in America. There has always been religious competition, even on board the Mayflower itself. And judging from all the failed attempts at outlawing it, there always will be. That is so, moreover, not because we have up until now somehow lacked the ingenuity to discover how to stifle religious competition. It is because it is impossible. There will always be religious competition because we human beings are conscience-driven creatures that have a built-in thirst for truth and goodness and find ourselves duty-bound to embrace and express the truth and goodness we think we know. Learning from our historic failures will also point the way forward. As we'll see, religious liberty is not now, and never has been, the recipe for eliminating religious competition. On the contrary, it is the built-in rulebook for how the game is played.

We'll also discover the roots of judicial confusion over religious freedom. At the end of the day, we'll see that, legally, religion in America is a lot like sex, race, or ethnicity in America. We don't deal with diversity by pretending we are all male. We don't deal with it by pretending we are all white. We don't deal with it by pretending we are all Irish. Why should we have to deal with religious diversity by pretending we are all agnostic?

OUR STORY SO FAR

The nickel tour of religion in America really does start with the Pilgrims. They just look a little different than they did in your second grade Thanksgiving pageant. For one thing, their halos need a little adjusting.

The Pilgrims came from England, yes, but largely by way of Holland. The leaders aboard the Mayflower had fled from England to Holland ten years earlier, and were no longer being persecuted. In Holland, they enjoyed all the toleration they could have wished for, and then some. Their great enemy now was assimilation. As their leader, William Bradford, related in his journal, "owing to a great licentiousness of the youth in that country," and to the "manifold temptations of the place," their children were being corrupted. In deciding to leave Holland for the American wilderness, they were not fleeing persecution at all, but permissiveness.

Nor were they seeking religious freedom in some abstract sense. They were largely after real estate on which to build their own little colony, a refuge where they could be free from the corrupting influences of the impure and could govern themselves according to their own vision of the truth. Think of them as Amish Calvinists. The great irony was that in order to be able to afford fleeing impurity, they had to accept the terms of the London financiers who were backing their adventure. Those terms included demands that the Pilgrims bring along with them experts in dealing with the various technical challenges a new colony could be expected to face. In short, they had to bring impurity along in order to leave it behind.

The result was a prickly voyage aboard the Mayflower as the "Saints," what the Pilgrims called themselves, squabbled with the "Strangers," how they referred to everybody else. It's easy to envision the scene. There, in the hold of a cramped ship, sat two stubborn groups, arms crossed, grimly eyeing one another. The Saints were dismayed. They had fled England for Holland, and now Holland for the wilderness, all to get away from impurity – and impurity had tagged along. Now what? For their part, the Strangers were glum. They had left their homes and their country not out of any great spiritual motive, but simply because this was the best job they could find. And, here they were, stuck on a boat with a bunch of holier-than-thou zealots. And soon they would all go off to live in the woods together. Great. Just great. How could this possibly work?

There, in miniature, is the question we still face: How do you live together with people when you disagree with them about what life means in the first place? The answer the Pilgrims came up with was vintage 17th century: the way to live together with people you disagreed with was by suppressing the heretics. Social harmony demanded a religious monopoly.

Throughout its early history, Plymouth Colony established state-supported churches, which all residents were required to attend and to support with their taxes. What's more, only members of those churches could vote or hold public office in the colony. But one could not simply join those churches at will. Membership was controlled by the churches themselves. The result was that, at one point in the colony's history, fully 3,000 people attended the official churches in Plymouth and supported them with their taxes. But only 230 of them could vote or hold public office. And when an Anglican cleric showed up and tried to organize a competing Sunday service, he was promptly deported.

Plymouth was also a highly controlled culture. The difference between October and December of 1621 is striking. In October, the Pilgrims held what has come to be known as the first Thanksgiving, an event that lasted several days and featured a modest feast, along with marksmanship contests and "other recreations." Two months later, however, "on the day called Christmas Day," Governor Bradford wrote in his journal, he called Plymouth residents "out to work." That was because, for Pilgrims, December 25 was nothing special. Christmas was, they thought, a "papist innovation," which they refused to celebrate. And since they didn't celebrate it, nobody else could either.

Now, not everyone agreed. Some newly arrived colonists objected that "it went against their consciences to work" on Christmas, so Governor Bradford grudgingly excused them "until they were better informed" and led the veteran colonists away to work. That arrangement lasted until lunch. Returning from the fields, Bradford was horrified to discover newcomers "in the street at play, openly" engaged in various sports. That is, they were doing exactly what the Pilgrims had done two months earlier. But this wasn't the Pilgrim-proclaimed Thanksgiving. This was that papist Christ's Mass. So the governor confiscated their sports equipment and told them if they wanted to celebrate Christmas "as a matter of devotion" they could do so privately in their homes, but there should be no "gaming or reveling in the streets." And so began, and quickly ended, the opening battle in the now nearly 400-year war over Christmas in America.

This was no isolated tantrum. A generation later, the colony formally outlawed Christmas for 22 years. (The English Puritans did the same when they seized power there under Cromwell. One result was the carol, "The 12 Days of Christmas," which sang in code—partridges and pear trees and so forth—of the 12 outlawed feast days between Christmas and Epiphany.) Once again, for the Pilgrims, social harmony required silencing competing religions, not just in their preaching and worship services, but even in their cultural efforts.

But if the Pilgrims were strict, their next-door neighbors, the Puritans in the Massachusetts Bay Colony, were positively ruthless. They were different from the Pilgrims. Where the Pilgrims just wished everyone would leave them alone, the Puritans wanted to be noticed. They meant for their colony to be the "shining city on a hill" that would so edify and shame the British Protestants that they would repent in sackcloth and ashes and become Puritan themselves, whereupon the Bay colonists would return to England in triumph. Needless to say, with that vision they could not afford to tolerate any heresy.

So when they heard of the Quaker movement that had erupted in England in the 1650s, the good Puritans of Massachusetts Bay grew alarmed. The Quakers, who recognized no religious authority except that of the Inner Light in their souls, were antithetical to Massachusetts Bay Puritans. The Inner Light had been known to lead Quakers in colorful ways, even requiring some of them to turn up naked at Anglican services, shouting "hypocrisy!"

The Puritans were appalled and decided to preemptively outlaw Quakerism in case any such people, naked or otherwise, ever attempted to come to Massachusetts Bay. Eventually, however, the Inner Light prompted a steady stream of Quakers to appear in the colony and to refuse to be silenced or deported. The good Puritans were aghast and met in session after session of their legislature, enacting ever more rigorous laws in an attempt to deter the Quakers. Nothing worked. First they held that Quakers who returned after being banished were to be severely flogged. Then, when that proved ineffective, they held that recalcitrant Quakers were, for a first offense, to have their left ear cut off, then, for a second offense, their right ear. For a third offense, they would have their "tongue bored through with a hot iron." That, too, failed to deter them. So the Puritan legislators passed yet another law specifying that itinerant Quakers were "to be banished upon pain of death." But not even that sufficed. So, on July 1, 1660, Mary Dyer, who had returned four times to preach against the Bay Colony (not counting the two trips she made to preach against the colony in New Haven), was solemnly hanged on Boston Commons.

The Quakers, though, still continued to come and to be hanged, until the King stepped in to demand an end to the executions. Mary Dyer's death certainly shatters The Myth of the golden age of religious liberty. But it does something even more important. It starkly poses a critical question: Why didn't she have it coming? The duly elected legislature had duly enacted the statute. She had notice of the statute. She knowingly and willingly violated the statute. She was lawfully arrested and properly tried. Why shouldn't she hang?

Of course, on its face, this is a preposterous question. You cannot execute people merely for preaching. True enough. But on a deeper level the question remains, why? Why can't you? It can't be that it was illegal; hanging her was legally required. It can't be that it was unconstitutional; there wasn't a Constitution yet. So, if Mary Dyer didn't have it coming, why didn't she? Isn't religious liberty just a legal question like any other?

Other early colonists, less homicidal (and more Christian) than the Puritans, had various responses to this question. Roger Williams, who founded Rhode Island after he had been banished from Massachusetts Bay, argued that people had religious liberty because it was the will of God. He was surely right, if ahead of his time. (The vast majority of Christians today would agree with him.) Unfortunately, his argument, based as it was on a theological premise, convinced only those who shared that premise. Put differently, when you announce that something is true because God told you so, you will naturally convince only those people who are prepared to believe that God talks to you. And, sure enough, Williams's vision of religious liberty lacked staying power. Within about a generation, new leaders of his Rhode Island Colony were barring Jews there from voting.

William Penn, the Quaker-founder of Pennsylvania, conceived of his colony as a refuge for persecuted believers of all sorts the world over. He even advertised for them in Europe. He too was appalled at the Puritans' logic. But he too had largely a religious argument for religious liberty, and it too faltered when challenged. Before long, the colony was demanding oaths and military service from even its pacifist Quaker citizens. Similar disappointments occurred in the other refuge colonies of Maryland and Carolina. There was a growing belief that people were entitled to religious freedom, as well as an ever more insistent question: why?

James Madison eventually answered the question, about a century later, in masterful form. Drafting portions of the Virginia Declaration of Rights, Madison wrote that people were entitled to religious freedom because of how they were made. "[R]eligion, or the duty which we owe to our Creator and the manner of discharging it," he wrote, "can only be directed by reason and conviction, not by force or violence; and therefore, all men are equally entitled to the free exercise of religion, according to the dictates of conscience." In other words, we are rational creatures who are required by our consciences to embrace what we believe to be true. And if we each have a natural duty to follow our consciences, then we each must have a natural right to follow our consciences. The Virginia Declaration made similar arguments for freedom of speech, etc. The principle for each was the same: there are certain fundamental rights that follow from human nature. These natural rights form the standard against which our laws are to be measured, and are not themselves created by the law.

That argument carried the day in the Virginia legislature during the spring of 1776, and Thomas Jefferson's echo of it, that all "are endowed by their creator with certain inalienable rights," carried the day throughout the colonies that July 4th. It was an argument that Madison and Jefferson continued to make after Independence—in both state law and federal law. Thus, Jefferson premised his Bill for Establishing Religious Freedom in Virginia largely on the idea that "Almighty God hath created the mind free." And Madison in his famous Memorial and Remonstrance against Religious Assessments in Virginia expanded on his earlier argument. He held that religion "must be left to the conviction and conscience of every man; and it is the right of every man to exercise it as these may dictate." What's more, Madison wrote that religious freedom was an "unalienable" right—a right that could not even be voluntarily surrendered.

Why? For two reasons: first, "it is unalienable, because the opinions of men, depending only on the evidence contemplated by their own minds, cannot follow the dictates of other men. It is unalienable also, because what is here a right toward men is a duty toward the Creator. It is the duty of every man to render to the Creator such homage and such only as he believes to be acceptable to him."

This argument was similar in its conclusions to the one Roger Williams had formulated. But, crucially, it followed from a different premise. Williams's argument was essentially a theological one: God had revealed religious freedom to be his will. Madison's argument was different. It presupposed the existence of the creator, true, but it was not so much an argument about who God is as it was about who we are. Madison's point is that from the contours of our humanity we can derive moral limits on the state's authority over us. So, our minds' built-in thirst for the truth and our hearts' built-in hunger for the good, combined with our consciences' insistence that we live according to the true and the good as we know them, have potent implications. They mean, Madison said, that we have the "freedom to embrace, to profess and to observe the Religion which we believe to be of divine origin." And, he added, they likewise mean that people who disagree with us must have the same freedom to follow their consciences as we have to follow ours.

Now, what is the practical consequence of declaring something a natural right? Well, among other things, it's supposed to remove the subject from the rough and tumble of legislative give-and-take. But things didn't always quite work out that way. Legislators could be fickle back then, too. And there was a certain cognitive dissonance about rights even from the beginning. Jefferson was shrewd enough to realize that. So, in a celebrated postscript to his Bill for Establishing Religious Freedom, he wrote that, while one legislature obviously could not effectively "restrain the acts of succeeding" ones, this law would "declare" that any future legislation "to repeal . . . or to narrow" it would "be an infringement of natural right." In other words, since he couldn't force future legislators to respect natural rights, he would try to shame them into it. Then, as now, sometimes that worked and sometimes it didn't. There were other struggles as well, notably the thorny question of how to secure natural rights in a federal constitution that left most authority completely in the hands of the individual states to begin with.

The result was a muddle. The framers alluded to natural rights in the Preamble, which speaks of "securing" the "blessings of liberty." And in the 18th century, "blessings" was not a term thrown about lightly. "Blessings" did not appear by some sort of metaphysical spontaneous combustion: they were the gift of a Blessor. But the argument was muted. The Constitution spoke in lowered tones about religion because most of its drafters believed religion to be a subject properly regulated by state, not federal, law.

An easy place to see that point is Article VI, which deals with a variety of miscellaneous subjects. Two of its provisions concern religion and, ironically, are juxtaposed. The Oaths Clause provides that either an "oath or affirmation" will suffice for federal or state officials to pledge their loyalty to the Constitution. This was to accommodate the religious consciences of Quakers, who are forbidden by their faith from swearing oaths.

The very next clause, however, is the Test Clause, which forbids religious tests for public offices or trusts "under the United States." That is, it forbids religious tests for federal offices. What about state offices? Didn't the Constitution protect state office holders from having to take religious test oaths as well? No, it didn't. In fact, it couldn't. All but two of the original states themselves had religious tests for public office and wanted to keep them. So the Constitution couldn't be against all religious tests, just federal ones. The result was cognitive dissonance, as the rhetoric of natural rights overlapped with the give-and-take of legislative compromise.

Following publication of the original, unamended Constitution, Madison and Jefferson carried on a lively debate over whether to add a bill of rights. Each argued that his position would better protect natural rights. Madison thought that religious liberty would fare better with no bill of rights at all. His argument was a simple one: If you subject a natural right such as religious freedom to the legislative sausage grinder, the compromise that will emerge will inevitably be disagreeable. Better to simply appeal to the pure natural rights themselves. Nevertheless, Jefferson won the day with pragmatism: Such hopes were unreliable, he thought, concluding that "If we cannot secure all our rights, let us at least secure what we can. Half a loaf is better than no bread."

The process went forward, with Madison proposing drafts that would have had the First Amendment protect religious liberty from state as well as federal interference, only to watch them get shot down, one after the other. The same political realities that forced the original compromise in Article VI insisted on the same compromise in the Bill of Rights. So, when it was first enacted, the First Amendment banned only federal action. Individual states remained free to keep their established churches, if they wanted (Massachusetts kept its established church until 1832), or to have complete disestablishments (like Virginia), or anything in between if they wished. Congress was powerless to intervene. And so, because it could neither override a state establishment with its own disestablishment or override a state's chosen disestablishment with its own establishment, "Congress [could] make no law respecting an establishment of religion."

Similarly, the Congress was barred from enacting legislation that was uniquely disabling to members of certain faiths. That is, Congress could not do to Quakers what the individual states had done in barring their preaching or penalizing their refusal to take oaths or serve in the militia. Congress could thus "make no law . . . prohibiting the free exercise of religion." And the Free Exercise Clause, like the Establishment Clause, did not apply to state action but only to federal action. In 1842, for example, New Orleans fined a Roman Catholic priest named Fr. Permoli fifty dollars for violating a city ordinance that prohibited displaying a corpse during funeral rites. Fr. Permoli's defense was that the ordinance violated the Free Exercise Clause of the First Amendment. The Supreme Court bluntly rejected that argument, stating that "the Constitution makes no provision for protecting the citizens of the respective States in their religious liberty; this is left to the States' constitutions and laws; nor is there any inhibition opposed by the Constitution of the United States."

Now, natural rights theory was present in the Bill of Rights too, as it had been in the unamended Constitution. If anything, it was slightly more prominent. The Ninth and Tenth Amendments had been added specifically to deny the proposition that the rights enumerated in the Constitution were all the rights there were. So there was still a natural right to religious liberty. There was just no way of federally enforcing that right against state violations of it. Whatever else may be said of such a fine distinction, it was often drowned out in the popular din.

Left free to persecute if they wished, many states continued to crack down on minority faiths. Vermont, for example, required in its constitution that all state office holders must "hold and profess the Protestant religion," thus excluding Jews and Catholics, among others. Many state constitutions included similar provisions, and a majority would go on to add Blaine Amendments, which targeted Catholics for economic discrimination. There were religious riots in several cities, notably in Philadelphia (where both sides had cannon) and in Manhattan.

Perhaps most damaging of all was the cognitive dissonance that was engendered by continuing to use the rhetoric of natural rights while the states continued persecutions that by any measure violated those rights. Thus, for example, when George Washington wrote his famous letter to the Touro Synagogue, he said of religious liberty that "it is now no more that toleration is spoken of, as if it was by the indulgence of one class of people, that another enjoyed the exercise of their inherent natural right."

But as the next 150 years would demonstrate, Jews in America suffered official anti-Semitism to one degree or another in virtually every state, and this was considered perfectly lawful. So while toleration was no longer "spoken of," it was the best that could practically be hoped for. While natural rights were trumpeted, they were almost always disrespected to one degree or another.

WHERE ARE WE?

You might argue that those were the bad old days and that the Supreme Court has fixed the problem. And it has fixed it, but only relatively recently. Moreover, the cure can be almost as bad as the disease. In its zeal to ban state persecution of religion, the Supreme Court announced in the 1940s that the religion clauses of the First Amendment would henceforth be "incorporated" into the word "liberty" in the 14th Amendment, which had been enacted in the wake of the Civil War, and which provided that "no person may be deprived of life, liberty or property without due process of law."

At the time, it no doubt seemed an elegant solution. The difficulty that soon emerged, however, was that this worked a major amendment into the Establishment Clause, taking what had been merely a structural provision, one that decided which branch of government, federal or state, got to decide on certain issues, and transformed it into an individual right without ever changing its wording. Now, how do you interpret a law when the only thing you know for sure about it is that it no longer means what it says? Answer: you look for other sources of meaning to pour into it. And that is exactly what the individual Justices of the Supreme Court have been doing for the last 60 years since incorporating the Establishment Clause. They have not been able to settle on one stable meaning for the Establishment Clause. In fact, they haven't even been able to settle on where to look to find one.

Over the last 60 years there have been three enduring factions on the Court that have survived several complete changes of the Court's personnel. One faction (e.g., Douglas and Stevens) essentially looks to philosophical secularism to supply meaning to the Establishment Clause. An opposite faction (e.g., White and Scalia) looks to history.

Meanwhile, a third faction (e.g., Powell and O'Connor) seems to have looked largely at the ceiling, sometimes voting with the secularist faction and sometimes with the more traditionalist one. (It is too early to tell whether this third faction endures in the Roberts Court.) The result has been theoretical chaos, joined to practical iconoclasm. A more or less constant majority of the Court has remained committed to scouring religion from public culture, without ever quite knowing why it must do so.

WHERE DO WE GO FROM HERE?

What to do? My suggestion is that we should change our constitutional analysis and return to Madison's vision about the broader natural right to religious liberty itself. As for the Constitution, we should stop asking the incorporated Establishment Clause questions it cannot reliably answer and ask them of the Free Exercise and Equal Protection Clauses instead. The Free Exercise Clause, unlike the Establishment Clause, protected an individual right to begin with. It thus poses none of the difficulties for incorporation that the Establishment Clause does. Like the Speech Clause or the Press Clause, the incorporated Free Exercise Clause now bans states from prohibiting the "free exercise of religion" just as it has long banned the federal Congress from doing. Moreover, the Equal Protection Clause of the 14th Amendment may be used in a principled way to regulate government distinctions on the basis of religion, just as it regulates government distinctions on the basis of race and ethnicity. Race, ethnicity, and religion are all so-called "suspect categories." That is, they are all human qualities on which the government may base legal distinctions only under the most rigorous conditions.

The analogy to race and ethnicity would also provide much-needed clarity in the annual battles over Nativity scenes and menorahs, etc. Government cultural displays with religious elements could simply be treated the same way we treat government cultural displays with racial and ethnic elements.

March 17 passes in peace every year without Anglophiles seeking to forbid St. Patrick's Day parades as Irish supremacist plots. Similarly, African-American History Month goes peacefully every February without European Americans attempting to block it as a racist power grab.

No court would take seriously the claim that the St. Patrick's Day parade is merely a foretaste of ethnic cleansing to come. Nor would judges stand for an argument that African-American History Month is but the opening chapter of apartheid. Similarly, courts applying an Equal Protection approach to religious freedom could finally admit that Christmas or Hanukkah decorations are not the harbinger of a new St. Bartholomew's Night.

In short, Free Exercise and Equal Protection analysis together could protect individual rights while providing a level playing field for religious competition in a scrupulously principled way. Unlike the incorporated Establishment Clause, the legal language of each of those clauses still means what it says.

Would changing our constitutional analysis like that finally usher in the golden era of religious liberty? No, of course not. There would no doubt be unforeseen consequences here, too. Moreover, much about current free exercise law would also have to be reformed, so as not to reduce religious liberty merely to even-handedness. But it would be a big step forward, by taking a big step back from the Court's current search-and-destroy mission for religion in culture.

But there is an even bigger step we can take, and one that does not require us to change the Supreme Court's mind. We as a people must realize that not all solutions are constitutional ones. The Constitution, while it codifies some protections for religious liberty, does not exhaust the natural right to religious liberty itself. This is perhaps the more important insight from James Madison's thought. We have seen how he advanced natural rights theory. Now we should focus on how he thought natural rights relate to legal ones.

Simply put, Madison did not think legal, or even constitutional, rights could limit the reach of natural rights. Or, even more bluntly, the First Amendment does not provide all the religious freedom there is. On the contrary, both in the Virginia legislature, when he was battling a bill to provide public funds for the clergy, and later in life, when he was inveighing somewhat more quixotically against funding congressional chaplains, Madison did not hesitate to invoke a broader natural right to religious freedom against a law that was permitted by the state or federal constitution itself.

In his famous "Memorial and Remonstrance Against Religious Assessments," Madison was faced with having to argue against a bill that was clearly permitted by the religious freedom provision of the Virginia Declaration of Rights. Madison knew that only too well. He had drafted that part of the Declaration of Rights, and in his draft he had attempted to outlaw government support for the established Anglican Church in Virginia, only to see that effort fail. To Madison's chagrin, the majority of the legislature, though happy to declare a right to religious freedom, nevertheless had insisted on maintaining the privileges of the established church. Thus, Madison knew, perhaps better than anyone, that the Virginia Declaration of Rights, which did not bar state funding of even one church, could certainly not be read to bar the funding of all churches. The law was clearly against Madison's position.

Nevertheless, in the "Memorial and Remonstrance," he gamely argued that the natural right to religious freedom itself prohibited such statutes. And he carried the day.

Similarly, in his less-famous "Detached Memorandum," written during his retirement, Madison argued that government funding of congressional chaplains was improper. He thought it should be held to violate the First Amendment (a position that even the modern Supreme Court has rejected). Failing that, he said, funding chaplains should be discontinued because it violates the "pure principle," or natural rights of religious liberty itself.

The point is not whether Madison was right or wrong on chaplains. Rather, the point is that well after the First Amendment had become law he saw no problem with advancing a natural rights argument for religious freedom. Neither should we. We should take Madison up on his insight and insist on our natural right to religious freedom even where it is outside the protection of written law. This does not mean urging on the federal courts extra-constitutional bases for their decisions. It does mean, however, that other branches and levels of government may take into account legitimate claims for religious liberty in making their own decisions.

How would that work? Let's take an example. A frequently heard criticism of the Supreme Court's current Free Exercise doctrine is that it is so narrow it would not even protect a first-communion class from a summons for underage drinking. And perhaps that's so. But if a local D.A. should foolishly seek to prosecute children on that basis, other government entities could ride to the rescue under the natural right to religious liberty. The members of the Grand Jury, for example, could and should refuse to indict. The state court judge could and should dismiss any indictment they did bring as "shocking to the conscience of the court." The trial jurors in the case could and should refuse to convict in any case that made it that far. And, in all events, the local legislators could and should intervene in the nonsense, by passing legislative exemptions for underage sipping of communion wine and by impeaching the prosecutor. In sum, we need to reform both our constitutional law and our self-understanding. Religious expression—even from competing faiths—is not some sort of allergen in the body politic. It need not, and cannot, be outlawed. On the contrary, because the religious impulse is natural to human beings, religious expression is natural to human culture—and deserving of legal protection.

So, is there religious liberty in America? Yes, but not really because of the Pilgrims. And only partially because of the Constitution. What's more, once you resolve the cognitive dissonance, you find it's not really at the service of social harmony either, although it usually helps it. There is religious liberty in America because there are human beings in America. And human beings have natural rights.

Individual Liberty and Private Property

Paul Johnson

John Locke's defense, in his second Treatise of Civil Government, of a new political order devoted to upholding the liberty of the individual, emphasized the right of property as fundamental to a free society. And private property has been the first target of tyrannical regimes ever since. Paul Johnson, the celebrated English writer and historian, explains why.

The connection between political liberty and the individual ownership of property is one of the great certitudes of human society. It is carved in granite, at least in the English language, where the words "freedom" and "freehold" come from the same root and have impinged on and interrelated with each other through many centuries, from the most distant origins of Anglo-Saxon communities in the Dark Ages.

The propensity of private property to promote freedom functions only when ownership rights are enforced by the rule of law. In Greek societies, and in Rome after the overthrow of the Republic, private rights were subordinate to the public power, so representative institutions withered or never developed at all. It was a different story among the Germanic tribes, which began to settle in the British

Isles from the early 5th century. Among them—as we can surmise, although we have no direct written evidence—rudimentary forms of freehold were widespread, and leaders tended to take important decisions after consulting widely with freeholding followers.

This key conjunction becomes more specific when early Anglo-Saxon England emerges in the documents. The laws of Aethelbert of Kent in the early 7th century reveal the existence of large numbers of free peasants with a Wergild, or death value, of 100 golden shillings each. They are likewise to be found, in even larger numbers, though with a much smaller Wergild, in the laws of Ine, King of Wessex, at the end of the same century. At that time there are indications that freeholders met with local kings in the assembly known as the witan ("wise man," the title bestowed on its members) to make or amend laws. As Anglo-Saxon England was united, from King Alfred's day onward, the great Witena gemot (assembly of wise men) developed as the consultative council of the country, distant ancestor of Parliament and of the American House and Senate.

The Norman "Conquest," as it came to be known, and the arrival of a form of feudalism did nothing fundamental to change this connection between freeholding and constitutional government. Slavery had virtually disappeared in Anglo-Saxon England, and the Normans, who were themselves rooted in the relatively free societies of Scandinavia, did nothing to reimpose it, although various forms of unfree tenure persisted for many centuries. King William I's barons gave him, in theory, knight-service in return for their lands, which were not, therefore, strictly speaking freehold. But knight-service was gradually commuted to money payments, and once land was bought and sold on the market, however primitive, true freehold developed. The king's great barons met three times a year, at Christmas, Easter, and Whitsuntide, in the Great Council, to give advice and consent, this taking over the function of the Witena gemot. At a lower level, freeholders were summoned to serve on juries, to judge facts and give evidence, by which process law was enforced.

In 1068 William embarked on the Domesday survey, determined at the Christmas Great Council, when the King "held very deep speech with his council about [England]—how it was peopled and with what sort of men." The survey itself was carried out by expert commissioners, summoning local juries of freemen to provide the sworn facts, and was conducted and recorded throughout in a highly responsible manner, indicating that the rule of law was taken very seriously indeed. This is the first great recorded political and economic event in English history, and it shows the overwhelming importance of individual landed property in society and government. The Book itself (I have held it in my hands, and it is remarkably light, being written on parchment, not paper) was the first key State Paper in English history and is still the central pride and joy of the Public Records Office in London.

The King continued to rule in conjunction with his great landed freeholders for two centuries. When the central power was weak, as under the disputed reign of Stephen, 1130–54, anarchy ensued, teaching the lesson that individual ownership must be balanced by crown authority to ensure that the rule of law is upheld in courts capable of guaranteeing owners' property rights. The reaction to anarchy, under Henry II, saw the introduction of a formidable series of constitutional laws, which the King was careful to enact at a series of Great Councils, where the freehold landed interest was fully represented.

When royal tyranny, as opposed to baronial anarchy, threatened to upset the national consensus and the rule of law, as under Henry II's son, King John, the property-owning nation, which of course included the church and the emerging towns, was forced to come together to bring him to reason. This was the story behind the Magna Carta (1215), the second great event in the evolution of the English form of sovereignty. It was written in the form of a statute, which the King was obliged to sign, and all his leading men of property did likewise. It guaranteed every person's rights, according to his condition, and promised that everyone would be judged by his equals. It became the first of the Statutes of the Realm, which continue to this day, and is also therefore the prototype for the enactments of Congress.

From the Magna Carta onward, there was a tendency to enlarge Great Councils into parliaments, in which towns as well as the landed interests were represented. This sprang from the need to raise money to keep the King's Government going, for the King could no longer "live from his own" (i.e., from the Crown estates), so special taxes were imposed, and that could be done only with the consent of those taxed, i.e., the owners of property, whether real (landed) or mercantile and financial. The major freehold landowners attended Parliament by individual writ of summons, but they were joined by "Knights of the Shires," two from each county, elected by minor landowners with property not less in value than 40 shillings a year. These "forty-shilling freeholders" remained the basic constitutional unit in the country until the Great Reform Bill of 1832, and the 80 or so County Members carried more weight in Parliament than the burgesses from the towns. The latter were chosen by a variety of franchises, but all were based on individual ownership of property, and inevitably MPs from the richest cities—Bristol, Norwich, and above all London—carried more authority.

Parliament as a whole constituted a representative assembly of property ownership of all kinds, in which mere head-counting of persons only very slowly became of significance and was not formally acknowledged until 1832. Nations that adopted democratic institutions in the 20th century proceeded immediately to one-person-one-vote methods of election, rather than going through the intermediate stage—which in England lasted half a millennium—in which property ownership was the criterion for the right to be represented in Parliament. Perhaps this is one reason why such democracies have proved so fragile. For without property of their own, voters have no fixed interest in conserving the property of others, and therefore no reliable commitment to political stability.

The existence, in England, of a parliament based on private property ownership and forming a tripod of power—King, Lords, and Commons, upon which sovereignty rested—was in contrast to most European countries, and explains why the English-speaking peoples developed differently, especially in two respects. First, it enabled England to preserve the rule of law more surely. Even during the reign of Henry VIII (1509–47), England's nearest approach, in the whole of her history, to a statist tyranny, the King was always careful to proceed through Parliament, both in enacting laws that repudiated the papacy and Catholicism and in executing his wives, such as Anne Boleyn and Catherine Howard, and ministers, such as Sir Thomas More and Thomas Cromwell. Parliament might be subservient, but it still functioned and represented the consensus of property owners, so the rule of law continued to be upheld.

The question remained to be settled, however: was the King subject to the rule of law as much as anyone else? If the answer was "yes," then property was safe, protected by the courts. If "no," then it was insecure. In this respect the Stuart kings were quite clear that they were above the law. As Charles I put it: "A King and a Subject are plain different things." In effect he claimed he was not bound by the Magna Carta but could impose taxation according to his judgment of national need. This was the real cause of the Civil War of the 1640s, and the issue was posed even before it broke out, when Charles exacted Ship Money (to pay for the Navy) by his own decree.

The opposition to this unauthorized tax was personified in John Hampden (1594–1643), a Buckinghamshire landowner and member of Parliament whose family had been squires of the village of Hampden and its neighborhood since Anglo-Saxon times. He was a man of considerable wealth, and this is important, for it enabled him to take on all the power of the Crown and its lawyers, in a case that was fought through the courts high and low from 1635 to 1638. As Clarendon, an eyewitness, wrote in his great History of the Rebellion, his refusal to pay the tax and his fight in the courts made him a symbolic national figure, "every man inquiring who and what he was that durst at his own charge support the liberty and property of the Kingdom, and rescue his country from being made a prey to the Court." Had Hampden been a poor man, he could never have done it.

His example is a classic case whereby we need men of not only principle but also wealth to give principle the sharp edge of power. As Hampden himself said: "He would be content to lend as well as others but feared to draw upon himself that curse of the Magna Carta which should be read twice a year against those who impinge it." A century later, denouncing George III's similar attempt to impose taxes upon the Americans, Edmund Burke underlined the moral point beneath the financial issue: "Would twenty shillings have ruined Mr. Hampden's fortune? No, but the payout of half twenty shillings, on the principle it was demanded, would have made him a slave." Hampden's wealth enabled him to fight the case vigorously and make its details universally known, so that while judgment in 1638 went to the King by majority (the judges being divided), Hampden won a moral victory, and when the Long Parliament met two years later, one of its first actions was to declare the judgment "against the laws of the realm, the rights of property and the liberty of the subject." Hampden continued to use his freehold wealth to support freedom, raising a regiment of green-jacketed infantry when the Civil War began, and dying from wounds received at the head of it in 1643.

Rich men have continued to use their resources to fight unjust authority in cases where poor men have no choice but to submit. A significant case occurred as recently as the early 1950s, in Churchill's postwar government. The war had invested government with all kinds of extraordinary powers over persons and property, and Parliament was slow to revoke this. The Marten family, considerable landowners in Dorset, had been forced to sell land at Critchel Down in 1940, to the Royal Air Force. At the end of the war, Commander Marten, head of the family, asked to buy the land back. This was refused. Instead the land was transferred to the Ministry of Agriculture, which in turn let it to a tenant. Marten, a man as obstinate as Hampden and as wealthy, fought the case. He eventually got an inquiry, which, after much legal expenditure, found in his favor.

The whole affair was an example of bureaucratic arrogance. The Minister of Agriculture, Sir Thomas Dugdale, who had been misled and lied to by his civil servants, felt bound in honor to resign, and his parliamentary secretary, Lord Carrington (later a distinguished Foreign Minister), tried to do likewise but was persuaded to remain by Churchill, who was greatly perturbed by the bureaucratic tyranny revealed by the affair and promised to speed up the repeal of all such wartime infringements of liberty. Thus Marten not only got his land back but also won a much larger battle.

Sir James Goldsmith, the billionaire, told me not long before his death that he intended to devote his life and fortune to fighting instances of government oppression of individuals who were too poor to fight for themselves. Alas, he died, aged 65, soon after. Would there were rich men today ready to carry out his intentions, for the curse of bureaucracy has never been heavier, the number of regulations more numerous, or the cost of resisting any injustice more ruinous.

The second way in which the English-speaking peoples developed differently from their Continental neighbors was in using the principle of private property to further overseas expansion. This in turn enabled colonies thus founded to proceed from the start to govern themselves and found representative institutions. In Portugal and Spain, forerunners in the field, the state did all and financed all, and the crowns of the two countries treated colonies as the personal possessions of the sovereign, who retained all rights. The French crown, broadly speaking, adopted the same policy, until in due course, in a moment of madness, the Emperor Napoleon sold all that remained, the Louisiana Purchase, to the American government in 1803 for a paltry sum.

The English approach was quite different. The work of voyaging, exploration, and settlement was left entirely to private enterprise. Individual "adventurers" fitted out their own expeditions, as

Sir Walter Raleigh did with the first settlement of Virginia at Roanoke. More commonly a commercial company was formed, in which men—and women—took shares and divided the profits accordingly. Royalty might participate, but as individual shareholders, on exactly the same terms as their subjects. Thus Queen Elizabeth herself had shares in Sir Francis Drake's great voyage around the world, reaping a splendid harvest of profit. The settlement of both Virginia and Massachusetts was undertaken by commercial companies, setting a pattern followed for a century.

Never in the history of human institutions has the connection between individual property and individual liberty been so surely and openly demonstrated. Obviously, where private fortunes supplied the finance for the colony, private views would determine its government. To be sure, the companies operated under Crown license, and the Crown might appoint governors. But the principles of representation and self-government applied from the start. Indeed in the case of Massachusetts, the first constitutional meeting took place while the Mayflower was still at sea. The Crown did not have the money, power, or will to rule its American colonies, as Portugal, Spain, and France ruled theirs, and by the time it formed the inclination to exercise authority, in the late 17th century, it was too late: the American colonies were, in effect, self-governing. Then when George III and his ministers imposed the Stamp Duty, they were seen as acting as usurpers and innovators, overthrowing an unwritten constitution of immemorial antiquity, and the King could easily be portrayed as another King John or Charles I.

The wealthy men who financed the original settlements tended to be radicals in religion and in politics, those who believed in constitutionalism and representation. Many of them were prominent in Parliament in resisting James I and Charles I. Hampden himself, for instance, was one of the 12 men to whom the Earl of Warwick granted in 1631–32 a large tract of land in what is now the state of Connecticut. The colonists followed closely and profited from the events of the Civil War and its aftermath. In the running of the colonies, the connection between private wealth in land and personal fortunes and the holding of office was continually emphasized. The colonists noted, too, that when the English twice dispossessed the monarch, first in 1688, when James II was replaced by his daughter Mary and his son-in-law William III, and then in 1715, when the Stuart line was effectively replaced by the Hanoverians, the effective leaders in both moves were the great Whig landowning families, such as the Russells, the Cavendishes, and the Spensers. They turned a monarchy founded on the "divine right of kings" into one founded on the sovereignty of "the King in Parliament."

Impossible, then, to exaggerate the importance of that unique form of private property, the ownership of freehold land, in the progress of liberty among the English-speaking peoples. The connection continued in American history. The great majority of those who created the American Revolution in the 1770s owned freehold land, often in large parcels. They saw themselves as the natural successors of the landed gentry who resisted Charles I and raised troops of horses at their own charge to fight him. As one of them put it, "they rummaged in Rushworth's Collections [documents about the Civil War of the 1640s] to find precedents."

Outstanding among them was George Washington, not only because of his height (6'3") but also because of his landed possessions, which were enormous, and which he farmed and exploited with industry and skill, then and later, to make himself one of the richest men in the hemisphere. Washington took a landowner's view of the crisis. Of course he objected to "taxation without representation." But his particular objection was the royal ordinance, which might, if enforced, prevent Americans from occupying and exploiting land beyond the Appalachians. He saw that America's long-term future was in thrusting across to the Pacific and taking the entire continent. In his own way he was a "manifest destiny" believer, and that is why he took up the sword. He wanted to serve without pay, both as general of the forces and later, as president, because he believed men of individual wealth had a duty to defend and promote freedom—in other words, richesse oblige. He saw himself as setting an example for all property owners. Unlike Franklin, Jefferson, Adams, and Madison, he had a vision that went beyond mere liberty from England to a vast, property-owning nation, based on almost unlimited land. He had this vision because he had visited more of America than any other of the revolutionaries, and had penetrated further into it, so as to grasp its potential.

Historical experience shows that, at least in Anglo-Saxon societies, the possession of freehold land leads directly to participation in the exercise of power and the enjoyment of freedom. As America expanded inland, it adopted, and pursued on an enormous scale for over a century, a cheap land policy. Under this, millions of immigrants to America, arriving without property, were able in one generation to acquire by borrowing and eventually own without encumbrance sizable farms. This process was accompanied by, and also promoted, the extension of the vote, initially to some, soon to many, eventually to all male citizens.

Ownership of land, as the most politically significant form of personal property, continued to be the mainspring of the American economy, the impulse behind the growth of its democracy and freedoms, to the middle of the 19th century. But in the meantime, the Supreme Court under John Marshall, and the wisdom and energy of Marshall himself, had laid the juridical and legal basis of American capitalism, which in time produced a vast property-owning citizenry in America's burgeoning towns and cities, thus reinforcing freedom and democracy by ownership of nonlanded assets.

In many societies outside the Anglo-Saxon tradition the development of liberty and permanent representative institutions was impeded by the insecurity of ownership. It was not so much that private property was rare as that there was no guarantee the courts would defend it in opposition to the state.

Take the case, in France, of Nicholas Foucquet, Superintendant des Finances to Louis XIV and a younger contemporary of John Hampden. He amassed a great fortune and built the magnificent château of Vaux-le-Vicomte, using the team of the landscape gardener André le Nôtre, the painter Charles le Brun, and the architect Louis le Vau. He made the mistake of entertaining the King there and displaying its splendors. Louis XIV, envious and competitive, promptly had Foucquet arrested and imprisoned for the remaining 19 years of his life, confiscated all his property, and used it, together with the design team, to begin the building of Versailles. There was no redress in a regime where a mere lettre de cachet, sealed with the King's privy seal, could lead to perpetual imprisonment without trial, or exile.

Hence in France under the ancien régime the landed classes and wealthy merchants were seldom if ever tempted to use their assets to advance public liberties, taking rather the easy path of sharing the spoils with the royal government. The only hope of change was revolution, often leading to more oppression. In Russia the Tsar alone enjoyed liberty of thought and action, and his property alone was secure. There, too, where private property could not be used to promote reform, the foreseeable end was popular uprising and the massacre of the royal family. In present-day Russia, where the rule of law is not yet firmly established, the new breed of financial oligarchs, who have looted the country's natural assets and flaunt their wealth in international society, are scarcely more secure than Nicholas Foucquet.

Unfree regimes both in the recent past and today have employed a variety of devices to prevent private individuals either from acquiring substantial property or from using it to promote liberties. In both fascist Italy and Nazi Germany, currency controls and heavy punishment of any infringement of them, real or imaginary, were the favorite method. In Communist countries, the private sector had virtually no existence. That no longer applies in China, where huge fortunes are being amassed and many millions of the new bourgeoisie now possess substantial assets. But the absence of a rule of law that can be relied on to protect the individual and his assets against the state and the obstacles raised to prevent their transfer abroad keep private property tame and harmless—no Hampdens there as yet.

This is one of many reasons why China's progress to wealth and widely based prosperity is likely to be overtaken in due course by India, which enjoys the protection of the rule of law, first established by its British rulers, and where the rich can use their fortunes as they please, even against the government. For if private wealth promotes freedom in a lawful society, so in turn does freedom promote yet more wealth. The economic superpowers of the future will almost certainly possess private fortunes of every size, in abundance, and the legal protection that alone underwrites their value. They will also enjoy, as do the United States and Britain today, free institutions. That is the lesson history teaches.

And the lesson needs to be learned. It is widely assumed today that a country has achieved freedom once its citizens have been granted the right to vote. But one-person-one-vote democracy coexists happily with tyranny in many parts of our world. This is for two preeminent reasons: the absence of a rule of law and the restriction of private property to a small and often self-perpetuating elite. Those reasons are connected, as history shows. Only when property is widespread, and outside the direct control of the state, is the sovereign power truly subject to law. And only when there is a rule of law can private property spread among the people without the risk of confiscation by the state. Thus in Zimbabwe, where every adult theoretically has the right to vote, but where real power and property belong to the dictator and the leading members of his party, voting can change nothing. Elsewhere, where poverty is too deep, widespread, and endemic, as in many parts of sub-Saharan Africa, the political process is regarded with incomprehension by the impoverished majority, for whom survival is more important than government.

Even in the United States and Britain we witness a connection between poverty and a loss of trust in democracy. It is a grim fact that the poor are less inclined to vote than the affluent, and the

very poor most unlikely to vote at all. The problem is greatly aggra-
vated if extreme poverty is concentrated in an easily distinguishable
minority. Poverty, or more correctly the consciousness of poverty,
depends not just on income but also on possessions. The very poor
own virtually nothing, and to them the democratic apparatus of the
state is meaningless, if not actually hostile. When the propertyless
are a majority they either withdraw from the political process altogether or invest their hopes in some kind of radical revolutionary
change, hopes that call forth brutal repressive measures from those
who stand to lose from any change to the status quo. Either way,
freedom is the first casualty.

By far the best form of property, from a psychological and therefore a political viewpoint, is realty, or real estate, above all the home
in which the voter lives. Here the organic connection between freehold and freedom applies just as forcibly to the 21st century urban
masses as it did to people in Dark Age Europe. Since the Industrial
Revolution of the 1780s, total wealth has increased many times, and
is increasing faster than ever. The problem is its distribution, on a
permanent, self-sustaining basis. The phrase "a property-owning
democracy" goes back to the 1880s. In the century and a quarter
since then, some progress has been made in giving it reality. Priority was given, of course, first to the spread of universal suffrage,
second to establishing minimum living standards. A third, perhaps
the most important, object, homeownership, was pushed into the
background—and even impeded until recently by the belief among
socialists that the working classes were best served by publicly sub-
sidized housing to rent. This policy, whose social consequences have
been on the whole disastrous, has now been largely abandoned.

If we are to underpin democratic freedom economically, we
should aim at a society in which more than three quarters of the
population live in homes they own, or are in the process of acquiring.
In Britain the figure is over 60 percent, and in the United States over
50 percent, so the object is attainable. Moreover, when the great
majority of people own their homes, they are likely to be much

more resistant to an intrusive state and more tenacious about their rights.

I would like to see the great political parties bring the spread of ownership, and its defense, right to the center of their programs, and compete with one another about the way to achieve these objectives. In doing so, they will accomplish more for freedom than any conceivable legislation to further "human rights." The magic characteristic of property, especially its core, homeownership, is that it is not abstract but concrete. It is real, as the term "real estate" implies. Politicians have fought shy of the issue because "property" is associated with the few. But that idea is out of date. Property is now owned by the many, and ought to be universal. The true slogan for the future is "assets for all." And were all to enjoy assets, the chances are that they will enjoy freedom too.

Liberty in the Post-Communist World

Anne Applebaum

No assault on individual liberty in the Western world has been so radical and destructive as that carried out by communism. The collapse of communism provides a unique opportunity to reflect on the social preconditions of individual liberty and its ability to re-emerge from the ruins of the socialist state. Anne Applebaum is a Pulitzer Prize-winning author and a well-known writer on the history of communism.

A mong many other things, the year 1945 marked one of the most extraordinary population movements in Polish history. Hundreds of thousands of people were returning home from Soviet exile, from forced labor in Germany, from prisoner of war camps, from territory still under Soviet occupation. The roads, footpaths, trains, and especially railway stations of Poland were crammed full of ragged, displaced people as a result.

At times, the scenes in these railway stations were horrific to behold: starving mothers, sick children, entire families were camped out on filthy cement floors, waiting for the next available train, sometimes for days on end. In the city of Łódz, a group of women, members of the prewar Women's League—an energetic, liberal-minded, charitable, and patriotic organization founded in 1913—decided they had to do something about it. They regrouped and reorganized the league in order to help the impoverished travelers. In Łódz, and across the country, Women's League members set up "women and children's shelters" at train stations and staffed them with volunteers, doctors, and nurses. They began supplying travelers with hot food, medicine, and blankets.

Their motives, in 1945, were the same as the organization's motives would have been in 1935: charity and patriotism. Janina Suska, a former Women's League member from Łódz who is now in her eighties, told me in a recent interview that she remembers these early efforts as completely apolitical: "no one received money for charitable work . . . everyone who had a free minute helped."

In fact, the re-creation of the Polish Women's League in the desperate postwar years was a classic example of the workings of what we now call "civil society." A group of women were witnesses to a social emergency. Without being asked or paid, let alone ordered or coerced, they organized themselves in order to help people cope with it. None of them expected the state to be involved in their charitable activity. Certainly none of them feared the consequences. To put it differently: at this stage in immediate Polish postwar history, the women of Łódz still felt a powerful sense of individual liberty and personal responsibility, and still knew how to organize themselves in order to exercise those qualities.

That was 1945; by 1948, the Women's League would be well on its way to becoming something rather different. As the Soviet-backed Polish Communist party slowly took over the organs of power in the country, as it imposed its far more limited vision of personal liberty and civil society on the Poles, organizations like the Women's League gradually lost their independence. Volunteers became employees, working at the behest of state bureaucrats, paid out of the state budget. Their offices were no longer in homes or private buildings, but in state-owned buildings. Their leaders were no longer independent-minded patriots, but Communist party members, or at least party sympathizers. The Women's League was no longer free to choose all of its own activities, but was expected, among other things, to help organize May Day parades, to make posters, leaflets, and other Communist party propaganda, and to use its network to recruit Communist party members too.

Anyone who objected to any of this—anyone who refused, for example, to march in the May Day parades—could be kicked out of the Women's League, or eventually arrested. Not surprisingly, the organization ceased to be independent. And the women who continued to work for it ceased to have the same goals and motivations they had in 1945. They were no longer free agents, but bureaucrats, working in the service of the state and the Communist party.

I have simplified this story somewhat in order to make a point. Of course there were some women who continued to make use of the Women's League's resources for good purposes, particularly in later years. But I'm describing the organization's general trajectory because it is typical, precisely reflecting the fate of many other once-independent institutions in central and eastern Europe following the Communist occupation of the 1940s, and in the Soviet Union following the Bolshevik Revolution of 1917.

Nowhere was this massive suppression of civil society accidental: everywhere, it was deliberately orchestrated from above. In Hungary, some 1,500 organizations were banned by the interior ministry as early as 1946, following attacks on Communist party functionaries and police. Violence was frequent: in East Germany, a wide range of youth groups, including Catholic and Social Democratic groups, were forcibly unified under the banner of the Free German Youth, the Communist youth club, in 1948. Those who objected were often arrested, sometimes killed. Nor was it an accident that civil society flourished in moments of relative freedom: the Czech Boy Scout movement happily reconstituted itself during the 1968 Prague spring, only to be crushed again after the Soviet invasion.

Much the same pressure was applied to private businesses of course, as well as to individuals. Book publishers who did not agree to print a certain number of the Communist party leaders' memoirs might find themselves deprived of paper. Artists who did not join the official "Artists' Union" might not be able to buy paint. Writers who did not toe the party line were not published, and lost their right to vacation in the state-subsidized writers' colony. Some went on refusing to toe the line: a generation of Czech intellectuals made their living stoking furnaces. Others bent to economic and political pressure and conformed.

Although the nationalization of industry and the pressure on intellectuals made more headlines in the West, the removal of the right to form even a stamp collectors' club or an amateur theater group without state involvement probably had a more profound impact on a wider swath of the population of Communist countries over time. Without private ownership, citizens lost their ambition and work ethic. But without civil society, citizens lost the habit of organizing anything, whether economic activity, entertainment, education, politics, or charity, for themselves. To use the language of Edmund Burke, they lost the experience of the "little platoons," the small-scale social organizations from which public spirit arises. Or, in the idiom of Tocqueville, they were deprived of "associations" which "Americans of all ages, all conditions, and all dispositions con- stantly form" and which, Tocqueville believed, helped Americans ward off dictatorship. "If men are to remain civilized or to become so, the art of associating together must grow and improve," he wrote. By the same token, the enforced destruction of the art of associating in eastern and central Europe led quickly to a form of anti-civilization, in which all forms of human behavior were, in theory, controlled by the state and all independent institutions were under suspicion.

Although it might seem as if this all took place a long time ago, I am retelling this history because it helps to explain some of the moral and practical difficulties inherent in re-establishing indi- vidual rights and liberties in central and eastern Europe today. In a very short period of time, between the late 1980s and the mid-1990s, much that had been illegal in that part of the world became legal again. Once again, it became possible to speak freely, to organize

independently, to work for a private business or charity. State sur-
veillance was withdrawn; barriers to travel and investment were
lifted. At least on paper, citizens became freeer.

Yet the private, social, and charitable institutions through
which citizens had once channeled their independent intellectual,
political, benevolent, or athletic initiatives no longer existed. In the
case of post-Soviet nations, they hadn't existed for several generations; in the case of central Europe, they had been destroyed forty
years previously. Much has been written about the loss of the work
ethic in Communist Europe, but by 1989, the habits, customs, and
even etiquette associated with everything from the culture of a
responsible newsroom to the organization of annual charity balls
had vanished too.

Worse, some part of the population in virtually all of the ex-
Soviet bloc countries was, at least to start with, actively opposed to
their revival. In 1989, the notion of a newspaper that publishes arti-
cles critical of the government was bizarre, even suspect, to many
ex-Soviet citizens. The very thought of a school organized according
to a different philosophy from state schools seemed strange. The
idea that a charity could be funded entirely by private people was,
to many, unacceptable, even suspicious: what would be the motives
of the people who contributed? Political parties engaging in uncon-
trolled debate were the most terrifying prospect of all: the spectacle
of people disagreeing, in public, sometimes even shouting at each
other seemed disruptive, divisive, even dangerous.

It is also true that, in the absence of civil society, words like
"freedom" sometimes seemed like empty slogans. Prohibitions were
gone, but positive ways to invest your energy or develop your intellect
were lacking. You might be free to spend your time as you wanted,
but the state-run football club you once played with had collapsed
for lack of funding, nothing had replaced it, and your community had
forgotten how to organize football teams on its own. You might be
free to engage in politics, but political parties were weak, corrupt,
and poorly organized. You might be free to read what newspaper you

pleased, but many contained nothing but pornography and gossip. You might feel outraged about the poverty around you, but you no longer knew how to raise money to help.

With time, of course, many citizens of former Communist states adjusted to the new realities, grew accustomed to the idea of individual liberty, and enthusiastically began to rebuild civil society. Others, however, did not. Across the region, the size of these two groups has varied, depending on a particular country's history and culture. And, as it turned out, this has mattered a great deal. In the post-Communist world, citizens' attitudes to civil society have, to a surprising extent, affected the development of ideas about individual liberty, ultimately affecting the political situation of the country itself.

To understand this point better, it is useful to look closely at two examples, on the opposite ends of the spectrum. First, Russia, a country whose citizens have largely rejected the Western model of individual liberty as exercised through the institutions of civil society, and then, once again, Poland, whose citizens largely accept it.

For more than a decade I have been closely involved with a new, post-Communist charitable institution in Russia. The Moscow School of Political Studies was founded in the early 1990s by Lena Nemirovskaya, a Muscovite close to the old dissident movement, and Yuri Senokossov, her philosopher husband. Although this was an era of enormous optimism in Russia, Nemirovskaya's plans were modest. She wanted, in her words, simply to "civilize" Russia a little bit, by introducing her country's young leaders to the intellectual debates taking place in the West. Toward that end, she began organizing seminars for young Russian elected officials, mostly from the provinces, to discuss the meaning of federalism, the role of a free press, the means of insuring an independent judiciary, and other abstract issues. She invited Western speakers, with a special emphasis on practitioners rather than theoreticians: working journalists, sitting congressmen, active members of parliament, current and former European officials as well as a few political scientists and historians.

By the year 2000 or so, the school was considered a huge success. It drew funding and attracted senior politicians from across Europe and the U.S. as well as Russia itself. Because the school was nonpartisan and nonideological, its first Russian participants described their experience at its seminars with enormous enthusiasm, using words like "revelation." For some, it was the first time they'd ever heard issues properly debated, with two sides of an argument given equal time. For others, it was the first time they had ever discussed a philosophical question to which there was no right answer. For most it was the first time they'd met foreign politicians and journalists, and for everyone it was the first opportunity they'd had to ask them questions.

The school began to get a reputation for producing thoughtful and independent-minded "graduates"—but it also attracted the attention of the Russian authorities, and as the second post-Soviet decade wore on, the school began to run into trouble. Nemirovskaya began to receive regular visits from the FSB, the political police that replaced the KGB, and the school began to be audited by the tax and regulatory authorities. Her success in raising Western funds was considered extremely suspicious, her friendly contacts with foreign diplomats even more so. Once, her home was raided by mysterious "burglars" who stole nothing but an award she'd been given by the British government.

Clearly, what had been considered a success in 2000 was, by 2008, considered by some to be a threat, even a center of espionage. Yet the school itself had not changed: it had stayed true to its original purpose, the promotion of open debate. But its values were slowly being rejected by the society around it. The school was dedicated to the promotion of individual liberty and open debate, but it was operating in a society where the very word "liberty" had begun to take on negative connotations.

And not only liberty. "Free markets," "democracy," "free speech," all the things Russians had seemed to want in the early 1990s, were, by 2002 or 2003, being rapidly rejected by the public at large. In part, this was because Russia's leaders and their foreign friends—most notably the American president Bill Clinton—had erred in telling the Russian nation repeatedly that these ideals had already been obtained. Looking around at the first fruits of what the American president was calling "freedom"—"privatized" companies that had been effectively stolen from the state, newspapers filled with libel, rampant crime and corruption, an oligarchy that had mysteriously taken control of the country's richest assets— many Russians decided that if this was democracy, they preferred authoritarianism.

But the deeper problem lay in the nature of the people surrounding Vladimir Putin, the man who became president of Russia in 2000. Almost all of them came not just from the former Communist party, but, like Putin himself, from the former KGB. Given their education and their training, it was not surprising that the new ruling clan distrusted organizations like the Moscow School. Deep down, neither Putin nor his comrades truly believed that Russian citizens, left to their own devices, would or could make good political or economic choices. Instead, they believed that unless controlled and manipulated by the Kremlin, Russian citizens would fall under the influence of foreign powers and act under foreign orders. These authorities did not, in other words, truly believe in the existence of individual liberty at all, let alone civil society.

With this kind of mindset, the Russian authorities perceived the Moscow School—along with human rights' organizations, environmental groups, and of course new political parties—not as an element of nascent civil society, but as evidence of a secret network, probably involving Western spies. That view was echoed in the Russian press, which took up the theme of "foreign NGOs as Western fifth columns." With apparent public support, the authorities began to discourage, even to threaten, people like Nemirovskaya and to encourage the development of a different sort of "civil society" altogether.

In 2005, Putin himself declared that "thousands of associations and civil unions exist and work constructively in [Russia]. However, not all of them are concerned with the real interests of the people. For some of these organizations the main objective has become to receive funds from influential foreign and domestic foundations, for others the aim is to serve dubious groups and commercial interests."

While it's true enough that not all associations are "concerned with the real interests of the people," who is to determine that? The Russian state solution was straightforward: instead of independent groups, initiated by private citizens and funded privately, the Russian administration created a state-financed, and state-organized, "civil society," allegedly intended to serve the same purpose.

As it happens, I've run into this phenomenon too. In 2004, I was asked by an acquaintance to speak at a seminar on civic education for high school teachers, being held at something called the Institute for Democracy. I went, and gave a short speech on Western journalism of a kind I'd given many times at the Moscow School. Immediately, the audience attacked me. The first questioner asked me "why America supports Chechen terrorism." Another asked me how I, a representative of the *Washington Post*—"widely known to be a U.S. government-controlled newspaper"—dared to speak about the free press at all.

The audience went on, parroting the most extreme version of the neo-Communist propaganda that was then beginning to appear in the Russian press. Afterward, I asked the organizer to explain the origins of the Institute for Democracy. It was, she explained, actually an older organization, formerly known, in Soviet times, as the Institute for World Peace. Although it had a new title, it was run by the same director and still operated according to the same principles. It "taught" students to follow whatever government line was currently in fashion.

The perks proffered by the Institute for Democracy—a free trip to Moscow, free meals, probably a stipend—surely encouraged many of the participants, provincial high school teachers, to attend the seminar. But I suspect that they had made an ideological decision as well. They came from that part of society that misunderstood "liberty" as "libertinism," that believed economic reform to be the equivalent of economic chaos, and that preferred the more orderly world of state organization and constrained individual liberty to the messy, unpredictable, liberated world of private education and civil society.

Not all of Russia shared these views: Lena Nemirovskaya is still there, and she has many colleagues. But the opponents of individual liberty are currently in power. For those in power, the Moscow School of Political Studies was indeed a threat, even a foreign conspiracy. They welcome the Putin administration, with its increased controls on media, its dislike of democratic opposition, and its threats against independent-minded organizations, as a positive force for "stability."

Although Putinism is the post-Communist ideology that most explicitly rejects individual liberty and civil society, it is not completely unique. Suspicion and distrust of the new liberties could be found everywhere after 1989, and are around still. In 2005, President Vaclav Klaus of the Czech Republic voiced suspicion of Western-style NGOs because they promote agendas, of "artificial multiculturalism, of radical human right-ism, of aggressive environmentalism." Perhaps so, but who is to determine which ones promote genuine human rights, or reasonable environmentalism?

In Poland too the suspicion of liberty has been voiced. In the months following the launch of the new stock exchange in 1991, the market fluctuations were so unexpected that one exasperated investor wrote a letter to a leading newspaper, complaining: "This market goes up and down, up and down; can't the government regulate it so that it goes up all the time?"

Nevertheless, from the very beginning, Poles most emphatically did not share Russia's mistrust of independent organizations on principle. In large part, this was because Poles had maintained a very few independent organizations through the years of Communism, and had even, in the decade before the regime actually crumbled, developed some new ones. True, the Communist regime destroyed or absorbed all kinds of groups: the Women's League, the Boy Scouts, the Order of Malta, the craftsman guilds. But it was unable, or perhaps unwilling, to destroy the Catholic Church. As a result, the church played a role in Communist Poland that was unique in the Communist world.

This role was partly intellectual—obviously, church teachings presented a clear alternative to Marxist ideology—but partly organizational as well. When I lived in Poland in the late 1980s, I was told that if I wanted to know what was going on, I'd have to go every week to a particular Warsaw church and pick up a copy of the city's weekly underground newspaper. Equally, if I wanted to see an exhibition of paintings that were not the work of the regime's artists, or a play that was not approved by the regime's censors, I could go to an exhibition or a performance in a church basement. The priests didn't write the newspapers, paint the paintings, or act in the plays—none of which were necessarily religious at all—but they made their space and resources available for the people who did. Officially, there were no such things as "independent," privately organized youth groups in Communist Poland. In practice, they existed—there was even an underground, non-Communist scouting movement—often within the physical, if not the spiritual, confines of the church.

But if the church was the oldest and most enduring example of an independent, nonstate institution in Poland, the Solidarity trade union was no less important. Born in the late 1970s out of a populist workers' revolt against poor living conditions—in large part, the workers were infuriated by the propaganda of the "workers' state," which never conformed to reality—Solidarity grew from a small organization in a single shipyard into a national movement very quickly. Along with the Flying University—history and literature courses organized in private homes, outside the confines of Communist-dominated state universities—Solidarity became, for many of its ten million members, the first real experience in "self-organization" since the war. Even though it was destroyed, and its leaders jailed in 1981, the memory of that organization remained in the culture, and a small part of the underground remained active.

Finally, the fact that Poles had some freedom to travel, and therefore had some experience with trade in the 1970s and 1980s, also turned out to matter a great deal. The much-despised Polish "tourists" who streamed into Berlin in the late 1980s to sell butter, eggs, and cheap manufactured products in open-air markets collected not only capital—later invested in small shops and businesses—but also the experience of engaging in productive, self-organized economic activity, unsanctioned by the state. It may not be quite the same thing as founding a software company, but there is still a world of difference between the mindset of a person who buys and sells Taiwanese computer parts at street bazaars for a living and one who works as a Communist functionary.

And because there were probably as many of the former as of the latter by 1989 meant that the majority of Poles were not in principle opposed either to private shops or to private chess clubs, and indeed welcomed both when they began to appear. The post-1989 expansion of individual liberty was unthreatening, precisely because most people understood, from the beginning, that free choices would be exercised through the sorts of institutions that Poles already understood.

In some spheres, in fact, civil society rapidly flowered. The Polish version of the charter school movement took off in the 1990s, for example, and there are now hundreds of charter schools and independent schools in a country that had none fifteen years ago. Some were formed by the "Solidarity" wing of the teachers' union, which began founding its own schools just as soon as it became legally possible. Others formed under the aegis of the church, or of church organizations such as Opus Dei; thus did old traditions of civic engagement spawn newer ones.

Other kinds of institutions took longer to get started, as people struggled to understand the new system. The fate of the Polish Women's League is, again, instructive. By 1989 the organization was utterly moribund at the national level, and in the early 1990s it more or less collapsed altogether. No one any longer had any need for an "official" women's group whose main function had been to echo state propaganda. But a few local chapters—of which Łódz is the most notable—felt that some of the functions they served were still necessary. In Łódz, for example, the League offered free legal clinics to women having marital or other problems that they were unable to solve alone. At first, the League petitioned the government for money to support such projects, but with only minimal success.

But over time the League learned how to find new sources of income and support. Since Łódz is a city of textile mills, many of which have women employees, the League succeeded in convincing employers that its services were necessary. Donations began to come in, and the organization stayed alive. Having lost its independence, it has now regained it. No longer a national organization, and no longer a state-run organization, the Women's League in Łódz now has a genuine purpose, and the women who run it once again do so out of conviction, as they had in 1945.

Of course, there are still hazards ahead, both for the development of such institutions and for their personal independence, which inspire their creation and which they in turn promote. Again, I can cite my own experience, and my children's experience, at a Polish independent school in Warsaw, founded in 2005. Originally, the school's aims were very ambitious. Its headmaster wanted to offer, in addition to the standard subjects available in state schools, extra courses, designed according to students' interests and teachers' abilities—classical subjects such as Latin, extra languages, arts—woven into the day. In addition, the school wanted to involve the children in the community around them through field trips and projects.

The model works, but only up to a point. As it turns out, there are both legal and practical constraints, many left over from the Communist era, which the school must constantly fight. Teachers cannot teach precisely what they wish to teach, for example, as they are obliged by law to cover certain topics. The law even dictates how many hours a week should be spent on Polish language, math, etc., what the content of some of the courses should be, and the length of the breaks between classes.

The school also answers to the same heavy educational bureaucracy that has been in place for decades. When a particular teacher recently took the decision, for example, to move a child from one grade to another, the change had to be verified with a local "pedagogical council," which required a psychiatrist's report, writing samples, and an extended meeting. The legal presumption was that individuals don't know best, that teachers can't make their own judgments about students, and that a bureaucratic institution representing the state must oversee all such decisions.

As it happens, the teacher in this case was willing to go through the procedure and argue his case. But surely there are others who, faced with the time and trouble needed to get an official approval, would have given up. Ultimately, this kind of interference weakens the school and the teachers who are trying to create something new. The suspicion of independent organizations that is so prominent in Russia may be less widespread in Poland, but it persists among those bureaucrats whose jobs and worldview continue to depend upon it.

To some extent, the ongoing threats to freedom that still exist in central and eastern Europe are no different from those in the West. Any nation, however old and hallowed its democratic tradition, is capable of producing unscrupulous politicians who manipulate the secret services, steal money, falsify elections. These things happen sometimes in the United States, in France, or in Britain, so it is hardly surprising that they should happen in Poland, Hungary, or Ukraine.

In fact, the real test of a nation's stability and dedication to freedom is not whether citizens' rights and democratic procedures are sometimes violated, but whether anyone reacts when this happens, and whether anyone bears the political consequences. The deep dividing line in the post-Communist world is not, as some would have it, between Orthodox and Catholic or between Slavic and Magyar, but between countries whose citizens actually react to news of political misbehavior and those where they do not. Evidence that a politician has been involved in a financial scandal can harm the electoral performance of his party in Poland, the Czech Republic, and Estonia. Evidence that the Russian president's secret services poisoned a political opponent using radioactive material did not harm the reputation of the Russian president at all. The maintenance of civil society thus requires the free circulation of information as well as institutions that allow the public to put pressure on the government. Any trends that weaken the flow of information—whether increased controls on Internet use or extended state control over the media—or that damage democratic institutions will ultimately prove detrimental to the cause of liberty as well.

In the case of those central European countries that have joined the European Union, there is another, special category of threat. EU membership has, it is true, brought benefits, some unexpected. For the first time in recent memory, central Europeans are able to travel easily, cross borders freely, study and trade in western Europe. Providentially, the first two EU countries to open their labor markets to central Europeans were Britain and Ireland, thereby giving hundreds of thousands of people exposure to the two most open economies in Europe.

Nevertheless, the EU adds another layer of even more unaccountable bureaucracy to that which exists already in post-Communist Europe, and therefore another layer of rules and regulations designed to make life difficult both for independent institutions and for individuals. More worrying, though, are the threats that the EU's legislative momentum and cultural imperialism could pose in the future. What the philosopher Roger Scruton calls the EU's universalist, "secular 'human rights' agenda" is often diametrically opposed to the local and homegrown ideologies of civil society, particularly those inspired by a religious or patriotic philosophy. Rigorous enforcement of "non-discrimination" against homosexuals could, for example, come into conflict with the rules of Catholic organizations or the Boy Scouts, as it has done already in Britain, for example, destroying Catholic adoption agencies. As Scruton writes, "the ideology of non-discrimination is inherently hostile to the spontaneous forms of membership: and it is sweeping the old forms of membership away, putting nothing in the place of them save a new kind of dependence on the universal state."

Myself, I'm inclined to believe that resurgent civil society is, at the moment, strong enough to withstand this ideology: Among other things, the experience of being in the EU has itself given new members a certain geopolitical self-confidence, allowing them to maintain some distance from the European intellectual mainstream. They don't feel the need to slavishly follow all Western trends, since their status as a "Western" country is now secure.

And if the threat is still there—well, it's the same threat faced by others. Economically, central Europe remains weaker than its western neighbors. But socially, culturally, even politically? I'm not so sure. In the 21st century, liberty will still be threatened in Europe. But for the first time in many years, the East may be better equipped to defend it.

Liberty and the Judaeo-Christian Inheritance

Rémi Brague

The liberties we enjoy in the West were made possible by secular government. But what made secular government possible? In this profound exploration of our religious inheritance, the renowned French philosopher and cultural historian Rémi Brague shows the deep connection between Western political liberty and the Judaeo-Christian vision of man's relation to God.

In 1877, the British historian Lord Acton wrote two essays on the history of liberty in ancient times and in Christianity. They were meant to be the germinal cell of a general History of Liberty that he never wrote. By Christianity, he meant the Christian area, which we would rather call Christendom, meaning mainly medieval Europe as it developed in the wake of the Emperor Constantine's conversion. Lord Acton's insights remain extremely valuable, so valuable, as a matter of fact, that, even if I possessed the necessary competence, I could hardly wish to replace them with a deeper or more accurate account.

Instead I should like to supplement Acton's insights by studying religion rather than culture, i.e., Christianity rather than Christendom. Moreover, I will focus on the common ground of Christianity and

49

Judaism: on the books known to the Jews as the Tanakh (an acronym for "Torah, Prophets and Writings") and to the Christians as the Old Testament. These books remain the core of what we call, rather clumsily and for want of any better term, the "Judeo-Christian" heritage. I will deal with the New Testament in a more summary way.

TWO ASSUMPTIONS

I will take my bearings from two basic assumptions. The first is that liberty is not a merely political fact. It strikes its roots in a deeper soil, in the very conception of man and of God that underlies a religion, and even in the way each religion conceives of the interplay of God and man in history. People who considered themselves Jews or Christians may not have been faithful to the claims and obligations of their religion. In examining the Judeo-Christian inheritance, therefore, it will not be enough to describe the concrete activities of Jews and Christians in giving institutional expression to the idea of liberty. We shall also need to understand the principles that governed their conduct and the ideals to which they aspired.

Hence I will not discuss the passages from both Testaments that deal with social phenomena in which liberty and the lack thereof were involved, e.g., the laws on slavery. Slavery was in the ancient world a common practice; it was part and parcel of the economic system, and few people ever thought of criticizing it, let alone abolishing it. In the city of rebellious slaves led by Spartacus, there were still slaves. Little wonder that the Bible does not say anything totally revolutionary about it but contents itself with advocating a more humane treatment of slaves.

My second assumption is that the idea of liberty was not a sudden invention, springing into existence as part of the great intellectual revolution that we know as the Enlightenment. Although the call for liberty is regularly conceived as some kind of break with Christian ideas and ideals that allegedly held sway over the Middle Ages, this conception is far from the truth. Western liberty is a far older tradition, the sources of which are to be looked for first and foremost in the medieval period. Lord Acton already could point this out. More was done after him by students of the medieval legal tradition and of the conflict between the papacy and the empire, in which both sides, interestingly, chose as their catchword libertas, i.e., "freedom." I would like to go further back, to the very foundations of the medieval worldview, i.e., to the sacred books of the Bible. I will take them in chronological order. From time to time, I will compare their content with what matches it in the Koran, which draws on some biblical stories, and underline the peculiarities of the two sets of texts.

THE OLD TESTAMENT

We should not expect to find in the writings of the Old Testament anything resembling a philosophical concept of freedom. First, because there are no concepts in the Bible. Ideas appear there under the guise of narratives. Second, because, wherever liberty is mentioned, it means a social status, the status of people who are not slaves. The same holds true of Greek philosophers, for whom freedom meant the condition of a self-governing city and also that of its citizens, who, unlike slaves, were owners of themselves. The metaphysical idea of free will is hardly older than the Fathers of the Church and owes its first clear statement to St. Augustine. At the same time, an important idea of freedom is implicit in many Old Testament passages. We have only to make it explicit in order to perceive its closeness to our thinking today.

CREATING FREE BEINGS

When ancient Israelite sages reflected on the absolute beginning of all things, they put freedom at the center of the relationship between God and the world. The first narrative of the creation tells us that "on the seventh day God ended His work which He had made; and

51

He rested on the seventh day from all His work which He had made. And God blessed the seventh day, and sanctified it: because that in it He had rested from all His work which God created and made" (Genesis 2:2–3). This way of explaining the legitimacy of the weekly day of rest is grounded on the story according to which God, too, rested after His work: "It is a sign between me and the children of Israel for ever: for in six days the Lord made heaven and earth, and on the seventh day He rested, and was refreshed" (Exodus 31:17). The Sabbath is free time, time for leisure, for activity, i.e., for the activities that become a free man. The ancient thinkers, who lived in societies of slaveholders, drew a line between what becomes a free man and what we are compelled to do in order to keep things going: tilling the soil, building houses, weaving garments, cooking meals, etc. They named the latter servile, i.e., slavish activities, whereas the former, which alone were worthy of free people, deserved the name of "liberal studies" or "liberal arts."

Now, the biblical narrative of creation makes possible a leisure that encompasses everybody, not only slave owners. The Bible stresses the fact that the servants, too, are to be granted a day of rest: "The seventh day is the sabbath of the Lord thy God: in it thou shalt not do any work, thou, nor thy son, nor thy daughter, thy manservant, nor thy maidservant, nor thy cattle, nor thy stranger that is within thy gates" (Exodus 20:8–11). This is the social dimension of the Sabbath, which became the thin wedge whereby ancient societies were opened to the pursuit of liberty.

Yet there is more to it. The Sabbath has another, deeper dimension, which we could call a metaphysical one. When the Bible describes God as withdrawing from His work in order to enjoy rest, God is described as free. But the world is, so to speak, free from God's action too and is allowed to rest. God does not interfere any more with what He has created. On the contrary, He somehow sets His creatures on a free footing. His providence gives them whatever is required for them to be able to "shift for themselves" in the pursuit of what is good for them. The necessary outfit that enables a creature to reach its own good is what we call its nature. The biblical God does not create bundles of independent properties that He arbitrarily puts together or asunder; He creates things that are endowed with natures of their own. To be sure, God keeps whatever exists in being, for without His continuous will to maintain them, they would disappear. But He respects the nature of the things He has created.

By this token, something like freedom already exists at an elementary level, even before it becomes conscious of itself in man. Human freedom expresses in a human key a property that belongs to each creature: the property of existing and acting according to a nature of its own. Interestingly, the Koran, which repeatedly praises God's creative activity, does not mention the rest of the seventh day. As a consequence, it does not contain any law on sabbatical rest. A verse even discreetly criticizes the idea that God could get tired (L, 38). Mainstream Islamic apologetics (Kalâm) later built a whole worldview in which things, and even time, consist of indivisible units or properties that stick together because God creates them afresh, out of nothing, in every instant. Such properties don't belong together because they express the nature of a thing, but merely because God is accustomed to combining them. No created thing, not even a human being, has a nature of its own, from which it can, as it were, enter into free relations with its maker. All are forever subject to His will. To be sure, the biblical worldview agrees in putting God above any fatigue (see Isaiah 40:28). Moreover, the New Testament insists that God does not stop "working" (John 5:17). But the world that God works to maintain is composed of things that are endowed with a stable nature and that spontaneously act in accordance with it.

GOD'S ACTIVITY AS LIBERATION

The God of the Bible does not only leave freedom to His creatures. If those creatures lead a historical life, He sets them free by stepping into history. Liberty comes to the fore right at the beginning of Israel's history as the Israelites understood it. Liberty is the very definition of the people of Israel as the people of the Exodus. Israel is not the only people that a divine being is supposed to have led from a former abode or state of nomadic wandering to its present place of permanent residence.

On the contrary, this was considered to be a common phenomenon; migrations were seen as the work of God's hand. Yet the history of Israel is the story of a liberation. The conquest of the Promised Land is the last episode in a process that leads the people to an independent life. The people are said to have been freed from a state of captivity they suffered in Egypt. Whether this matches a historical fact is scarcely relevant. What is important is the kind of experience of God that is implied in such a narrative. When God introduces Himself to His people, He does what we do when we first tell our name, then the trade that we ply: "I am the Lord thy God, which have brought thee out of the land of Egypt, out of the house of bondage" (Exodus 20:2). God's job, so to speak, consists in setting people free.

Now, this introduction explains the meaning of what follows, i.e., the famous "Decalogue," which we commonly translate as "the ten commandments." But the word means more exactly ten utterances, for the very first one, which I have just quoted, is not a commandment but a self-description. Yet it provides us with the key to a proper understanding of the so-called "commandments."

THE CODE OF FREE PEOPLE

Those Commandments, be they positive or negative, are not expressed with the imperative particle ("do this," "don't do that"), but with the particle that invokes or negates a future tense ("thou shalt do this" or "not do that"). They describe the logical consequences of the liberation wrought by God. We have to understand: because you are now free people, you won't have to do any more what slaves do, i.e., you won't kill, you won't steal, etc. The word "commandment" has a ring of submission. But the Decalogue is not about submission at all. What we call the laws is the codification of liberty. The laws don't limit freedom by setting rules that we are not allowed to trespass. Abiding by the law is nothing more than remaining faithful to the logic of liberation, taking one's freedom seriously and drawing whatever consequences it might have. In fact, the "commandments" are something like the code of honor of free people, of gentlemen who are aware of "what is not done." They connect the gift of freedom with the responsibilities that naturally flow from it.

With some irony, we could interpret many features of the Ten Commandments in the light of aristocratic ethics: a gentleman does not bow down to a graven image nor serve it (Exodus 20:5); a gentleman does not tell fibs (v. 7, 16); he does not toil all the time but grants himself and his manservants a day of rest (v. 8–10); he honors his lineage (v. 12); he does not mingle in dirty business like killing, betraying his wife, or pilfering (v. 13–15); he does not even stoop to look at other people's property (v. 17), etc. On the other hand, the liberty that the people of Israel enjoy is not that of the aristocratic libertine. The trouble with born gentlemen is that even if they indulge in the most shameful vices, they will do so with perfect grace and propriety, like Mozart's Don Juan, never losing their exquisite distinction and manners. As a consequence, they won't be particular about morality. Even if they "play the game," they won't take such things too seriously when none of their peers are watching. On the other hand, people who retain the gnawing consciousness of being, at the end of the day, mere upstarts, will normally react by behaving in a more gentlemanly way than "real" gentlemen. They will even slightly overdo things, just to be on the safe side. We can spot something like that in ancient Israel, especially among the prophets.

LIBERTY FOR THE SLAVES

Israel's past liberation from Egypt is constantly brought to memory as a gift, so that liberty cannot be separated from the consciousness of a former bondage. This unpleasant remembrance is almost harped upon: "And remember that thou wast a servant in the land of

Egypt, and that the Lord thy God brought thee out thence through a mighty hand and by a stretched out arm: therefore the Lord thy God commanded thee to keep the Sabbath day" (Deuteronomy 5:5). This has consequences for the behavior that is expected of the Israelite toward foreigners: "Thou shalt neither vex a stranger, nor oppress him: for ye were strangers in the land of Egypt" (Exodus 22:21; see Deuteronomy 10:19). Because liberty is nothing natural, but something that was vouchsafed by God, being born a free man loses its relevance, and the difference between true-blue Israelites and the others is played down: "But the stranger that dwelleth with you shall be unto you as one born among you, and thou shalt love him as thyself; for ye were strangers in the land of Egypt" (Leviticus 19:34). Also "thou shalt not oppress a stranger: for ye know the heart of a stranger, seeing ye were strangers in the land of Egypt" (Exodus 23:9).

Hence biblical liberty is not peacefully enjoyed by a privileged caste. It exists in a dynamic dimension: it must be shared with other people and expanded to the whole of mankind. Freedom introduces a dynamic of liberation. The Bible generalizes aristocratic ethics to a people in its entirety. This may have something to do with a fact that had momentous consequences in Western political theory: the legitimacy of monarchic rule was always implicitly qualified, and often explicitly attacked. Such a critical stance toward monarchy was a new phenomenon. In the ancient world, we find from time to time critiques leveled at this or that concrete ruler. More than one Roman emperor was portrayed by Tacitus as a bloodthirsty tyrant and lampooned by Suetonius because of his deviant sexual practices. We find reflections on the respective value of the various political regimes, e.g. in Herodotus, who reports in his Histories (III, 80–82) the discussion that allegedly took place between the supporters of those regimes after a revolution did away with an impostor. The upshot was the choice of monarchy.

The Bible is the only ancient text that contains a critique of monarchy as such, not of this or that concrete king, not as pitted against another political system (I Samuel 8:10–18). The only legitimate rule is supposed to be God's direct rule. This is not a claim in favor of theocracy, if we mean thereby the rule of priests over lay people. It is an appeal to everybody to behave as a priest, as Israel is "a nation of priests" (Exodus 19:6).

FREE DISCUSSION WITH GOD

The way in which God behaves with His people shows that the Lord Himself respects the freedom of His creatures. This comes to the fore in a scene that several prophets, among the most ancient, repeatedly put on stage: the God of Israel is supposed to have with His unfaithful people a lover's tiff, and even to bring a lawsuit (Hebrew rîv) against them. Thus Hosea, a prophet of the Northern Kingdom of Israel in the eighth century BCE, declares: "Hear the word of the Lord, ye children of Israel: for the Lord hath a controversy with the inhabitants of the land, because there is no truth, nor mercy, nor knowledge of God in the land. By swearing, and lying, and killing, and stealing, and committing adultery, they break out, and blood toucheth blood" (Hosea 4:1–2). Likewise Isaiah, a prophet of the Southern Kingdom of Judah in the same period, announces that "the Lord standeth up to plead, and standeth to judge the people. The Lord will enter into judgment with the ancients of His people, and the princes thereof: for ye have eaten up the vineyard; the spoil of the poor is in your houses. What mean ye that ye beat my people to pieces, and grind the faces of the poor? saith the Lord God of hosts" (Isaiah 3:13–15).

The reasons for God's wrath and desire to litigate with His people have nothing to do with God's own "interests" (supposing this could make any sense), but very much to do with the good of those who most urgently need protection, i.e., the poor. There is a particularly revealing passage in Micah, another prophet from the eighth-century BCE Kingdom of Judah: "Hear ye now what the Lord saith: Arise, contend thou before the mountains, and let the hills hear thy voice. Hear ye, O mountains, the Lord's controversy, and ye strong foundations of the earth: for the Lord hath a controversy with His people, and he will plead with Israel. O my people, what have I done unto thee? And wherein have I wearied thee? Testify against me. For I brought thee up out of the land of Egypt, and redeemed thee out of the house of servants; and I sent before thee Moses, Aaron, and Miriam" (Micah 6:1–4). The powers of nature are called to witness. They are described according to the worldview that prevailed at that time: the earth is seen as a flat surface posited on pillars. But discarding this as obsolete would let an important element go: God and the people are not facing one another. There is a third character in the drama, before which their dispute is being judged. In this case, the part is played by mountains, hills, and the primeval abyss. We would call this character by a name that is lacking in the Old Testament: "nature."

In short, we have entered the realm of law. The dimension of the juridical begins when two litigants contend in the presence of a third, neutral person. God argues with His people on the basis of commonly received moral principles. Those principles are not simply what God happens to will. They exist by what later thinkers will call "nature." There is a common ground of basic decency between God and man, a ground on which man can stand even without an explicit knowledge of the God of Israel. This is what Hosea calls "knowledge of God" in the passage quoted above: the "god" there has capital letters for the translators only. "Knowing God" or "fearing God" means hardly more than abiding by the rules of common decency (see Genesis 20:11).

The Koran does not mention such scenes. The recurrent pattern is: God sends a prophet to a human group and commands that something should be done or avoided; He is not obeyed; the disobedient group is utterly destroyed by some device: a strong wind, an earthquake, a flood, etc. (XXIX, 40.) To be sure, many contradictory discussions between the prophets and their people are reported, but none take place between God and the prophets whom He sends. Exchange takes place only between beings that exist on the same level. God does not admit any bargain with Him. Little wonder that Abraham's famous haggling with God about the fate of Sodom (Genesis 18:22–33) is quickly alluded to but not told (XI, 74).

EXPECTING

The fifth chapter of Isaiah opens with a well-known song: "Now will I sing to my well-beloved a song of my beloved touching his vineyard. My well-beloved hath a vineyard in a very fruitful hill: And he fenced it, and gathered out the stones thereof, and planted it with the choicest vine, and built a tower in the midst of it, and also made a winepress therein: and he looked that it should bring forth grapes, and it brought forth wild grapes. And now, O inhabitants of Jerusalem, and men of Judah, judge, I pray you, betwixt me and my vineyard. What could have been done more to my vineyard, that I have not done in it? wherefore, when I looked that it should bring forth grapes, brought it forth wild grapes?" (Isaiah 5:1–4).

The allegory is quickly explained. God's vineyard is the country of Israel, the vine is the people, the fruit stands for the latter's deeds, good or bad. The whole passage belongs to the literary genre of the lawsuit between God and His people: the Israelites are summoned to judge between God and the vine, viz. themselves. Their guilt is, as always, moral in nature: They have denied justice, taken bribes, and so on. The interesting point, however, is the attitude of God. He does not command the vine to produce good grapes. This is what the vine is expected to do (God "looks that . . ."), because this is what a vine, when it is properly looked after, normally and spontaneously does. To use a nonbiblical word, it is the nature of the vine to produce grapes. In the same way, God does not, properly speaking, command righteous moral behavior. How one should behave is already a matter of common knowledge, which can be brought back to the memory, but not taught. God expects moral behavior to spring forth from human nature, and to spring forth freely.

THE NEW TESTAMENT

The New Testament takes for granted the whole content of the Old. But it was written in cultural surroundings that, unlike ancient Israel, were familiar with conceptual thought. The Greek in which it was written knows the word for "freedom" (*eleutheria*). Neverthe-less, freedom is there not only where the word is present but also where it is not. Jesus's death, which took place on Easter eve, and his resurrection are thought of on the model of the former Easter, Israel's liberation from Egyptian bondage, hence as a new exodus. When Luke's Gospel tells us about the Transfiguration on the Mount (9:31), it explains that Jesus spoke with Moses and Elias about his "departure." The word used is the Greek "exodos," in a clear allusion to the first exodus. Jesus's passion is conceived of as setting man free from a captivity that affects man more deeply than the one the people experienced in Egypt, the captivity of sin.

Sin has been conceived of by philosophers and religious people in various ways: as offending God, as trespassing against a rule, as sullying the purity of our soul, as increasing the burden that chains us to the wheel of samsara and condemns us to reincarnation, etc. The New Testament sees sin first and foremost as a weakening of our own liberty.

Liberty is the goal of the liberation wrought by Christ. "Stand fast therefore in the liberty wherewith Christ hath made us free, and be not entangled again with the yoke of bondage" (Galatians 5:1). The Revised Standard Version has, more literally: "For freedom Christ has set us free." The ultimate aim of such a liberation is not leaving one master and falling prey to another. It is the full expression of what we naturally are. The ultimate goal of salvation, mankind's ultimate hope, is conceived as total freedom: "the creature itself also shall be delivered from the bondage of corruption into the glorious liberty of the children of God" (Romans 8:21).

HISTORY AS THE REALM OF LIBERTY

A passage from Paul draws the whole picture of the way God respects freedom in His dealings with man. It is the grandiose beginning of the Epistle to the Ephesians: "Blessed be the God and Father of our Lord Jesus Christ, who hath blessed us with all spiritual blessings in heavenly places in Christ: According as He hath chosen us in Him before the foundation of the world, that we should be holy and without blame before Him in love: Having predestinated us unto the adoption of children by Jesus Christ to Himself" (1:3–5). The originality of the New Testament outlook becomes still more spectacular when we compare this passage with a verse from the Koran: "And (remember) when thy Lord brought forth from the Children of Adam, from their reins, their seed, and made them testify of themselves, (saying): Am I not your Lord? They said: Yea, verily. We testify. (That was) lest ye should say at the Day of Resurrection: Lo! of this we were unaware, or lest you should say: It was our fathers who associated partners with Allah" (VII, 172). The common point is the fact that the scene is supposed to have taken place before the creation of the world, or at least of mankind, in the highest heavens. The big difference lies in man's answer. In the Koran, it is given immediately afterward by Adam's posterity, miraculously put in its entirety in front of God. The whole of mankind has pledged allegiance to its Creator, and accepted, even before mankind's existence, the fundamental doctrine of the Koran, that God is one, without partners. This has positive and negative consequences. Positively, every son of Adam, i.e., each and every human being, has submitted to God from the outset. Islam (submission) is therefore the original and "natural" religion of mankind, whereas, according to a frequently quoted utterance of Muhammad (hadith), the other religions are foisted upon children by their parents. Islam is the religion into which each child is born. This explains why no formal act of joining the community of believers, such as the Christian baptism, is required.

On the negative side, disobedience cannot be excused. The lack of submission to God's will is not tough luck, or an error, or a simple moral failure; it is a kind of treason. It involves falling away from a religion that was implanted in all of us by the Creator. Not only does Islam forbid apostasy, therefore, as an inexcusable offence; it has a tendency to regard the adherents of other faiths as already apostates, guilty of the primary sin against God.

In the Epistle to the Ephesians, a question is implicitly asked: Will mankind accept God's benediction and the whole plan of salvation that it implies? But the answer is not given. Of course, God expects that man will react positively and accept the offer. But in the time that stretches before the creation of the world nothing whatsoever takes place, except God's initiative. What actually happens, including any possible answer of man, does so in history.

History is the very answer. But it is an open one; nobody knows whether the answer of mankind will be, in the long run, positive or negative. We can only hope that "all manner of things will be well." History is the stage on which the drama of liberty is played.

CONCLUSION

What cultures that were influenced by the Jewish and Christian religions made of the ideal of liberty that I have been finding in both Testaments is a task for historians. Impartial historians will observe how miserably the ideal and its realization often jarred with each other. On the other hand, they will have to acknowledge that free institutions hardly ever developed in places that were not influenced by Jewish and Christian ideas. Outside the Judeo-Christian tradition, it has been rare for thinkers to suppose that God endowed us with a nature of our own, that freedom is part of that nature, and that it is through the exercise of freedom, and the errors that inevitably stem from it, that we fulfill God's plan. The mainstream tradition of Islam has certainly regarded freedom, both personal and political, as valuable—but valuable largely as a means to submission. And when Lord Acton tells us that "liberty is not a means to a higher political end; it is itself the highest political end," he is echoing voices that can be heard in all the sacred books of our tradition, from the Torah to the Epistles of St. Paul.

Individual Liberty as the Constitution Understands It

Robert Bork

The Constitution of the United States is universally recognized as an expression of the Enlightenment, in which wise and prescient men embodied their aspirations for a society in which the individual would be sovereign and free. Under pressure from liberal activism, however, the Constitution is now interpreted in a way that the Founders would never have intended. Judge Robert Bork, America's best-known exponent of conservative jurisprudence, explains the consequences for individual liberty.

To consider liberty in relation to the Constitution is to enter a subject of some ambiguity. Which Constitution are we to consider? The document has undergone dramatic shifts in its coverage and in its meaning over the course of our history. The unamended document ratified in 1787 had little explicit to say about individual liberties. Aside from provisions such as those barring states from discriminating against persons from other states, bills of attainder, ex post facto laws, and the suspension of the writ of habeas corpus without the consent of Congress, individual liberty was to be protected by the structure of the federal government. The states were largely left to deal with issues of liberty as they saw fit.

The Federalists, who favored the proposed Constitution, regarded its structural features as crucial. As James Madison pointed out in his famous tenth essay in *The Federalist*, the primary source of danger was the propensity of men to form factions, enabling a majority to oppress minorities. He argued that the sheer size of the population, coupled with the diversity of commercial interests, would make it harder for a national majority faction to form. Other safeguards were the enumeration of powers to which the national government would be confined (a false hope), and the provision of different terms of office for the president, the Senate, and the House of Representatives. Different election dates would supposedly make the formation of stable majority factions very difficult.

The anti-Federalists were, or said they were, dissatisfied with these protections. They demanded a Bill of Rights as well. Some of them apparently were less interested in a Bill for its own sake than in citing its absence as a reason to reject the Constitution. To counter that tactic, the Federalists promised that a Bill of Rights would be put forward promptly after ratification of the main document. The anti-Federalists expressed fear that the unamended Constitution would allow the rise of an "aristocracy." What they did not foresee was that the meaning of the Bill of Rights would alter dramatically with changes in the political and cultural climate. Thus, it is one of the ironies of our history that it was the adoption of a Bill of Rights in 1791, together with the establishment of judicial review in *Marbury v. Madison* (1803), and the subsequent application of the Bill of Rights to the states through the 14th Amendment, that ultimately led to a virtually omnipotent aristocracy, one that has rewritten major features of the Constitution, including the Bill of Rights itself.

It is true, of course, that radical changes affecting individual liberty have occurred with respect to congressional powers enumerated in Article I, Section 8 of the Constitution. But those changes are different in kind and origin than those displayed in the alterations of the meaning of the Bill of Rights. The idea of confining Congress to the enumerated powers of Article I, Section 8 (an idea reinforced by the 10h Amendment) is dead and cannot be revived. Contrary to some conservative fantasies, federalism was not killed by New Deal justices who perverted this aspect of the Constitution but by the American people and the realities of national politics. The public wants a large and largely unrestrained national government, one capable of giving them what they want, irrespective of the limitations inherent in the enumeration of powers, and they will, sooner or later, get justices who will allow them such a government. The great engine of constitutional reform is mortality. (The boast that our Constitution has lasted for more than 200 years is largely empty. In no branch of government—legislative, executive, or judicial—are we living under the Constitution and the first 10 amendments as these were understood when ratified, respectively, in 1787 and 1791.) The decline of federalism as a judicially enforced doctrine has had profound effects on individual liberty, both positive and negative. When states were the primary source of legislation, persons who found the laws oppressive could migrate to other states to gain additional freedom. Although that was true in many aspects of life, perhaps the most obvious instance was the migration of blacks from southern to northern states during and after World War II. It was close to an impossibility to avoid *federal* law by migrating.

Not everybody could move state to state, however, and federalism, under the name of "states' rights," was used for years to block national civil rights legislation, frustrating attempts to improve the individual liberties of black citizens. Federal intervention outlawed the Black Codes of the South and, applying the 1964 Civil Rights Act through a very expansive reading of the Commerce Clause, did much to ban even private racial discrimination. Today, the vitality of federalism is reduced to the occasional limitation of some federal power that has absolutely no relation to an enumerated power. Such cases tend to be trivial. Obviously, the invocation of federalism in such circumstances is mainly symbolic, an almost nostalgic celebration of constitutional law as originally envisaged.

The Bill of Rights continues to have far more visible relevance to individual liberties than do the structural safeguards stressed by Madison. The Bill serves, moreover, as a weather vane, reflecting the beliefs and moods of the dominant social class of the time. It seems in our early history not to have been important in either function, for it lay unused by the Supreme Court until 1856. Perhaps that was because the Bill of Rights was not taken terribly seriously at the outset. Thomas Jefferson treated it cavalierly enough. When it was adopted, his report of events to the governor of Virginia placed it after fairly trivial matters, such as the authorization of some lighthouses.

Joseph Story's acclaimed *Commentaries on the Constitution of the United States* (1833) gives the Bill of Rights only the most cursory description, hardly more than a repetition of the text. The Bill played little or no role in the courts and only belatedly entered the political debate over the Alien and Sedition Act. Jefferson's first response was that the suppression of political speech was the function of the states rather than the national government, although he ultimately shifted his argument to the First Amendment's guarantee of free speech.

The Bill of Rights made a disastrous debut in the Supreme Court in 1856 with *Dred Scott v. Sandford*, which invented a constitutional right to own slaves that could be asserted against the federal government. This was based, among other things, on the Due Process Clause of the Fifth Amendment. This was what we would call today a decision by judicial activists, which means that it was not plausibly related to the actual text or history of the Constitution. Because the decision is perhaps best explained by the fact that seven of the nine justices were southerners, *Dred Scott* does not tell us a great deal about individual liberty as the Constitution then understood it. The activist decisions that followed the Civil War—this time directed against state legislation—reveal more.

After *Dred Scott,* the Bill of Rights and the 14th Amendment were relatively quiescent until the latter third of the 19th century and the early 20th century, when occasional decisions upheld the liberties of businesses, defined as freedom from vexatious economic regulations. Although the idea of liberty, in one of its many forms, lies behind various decisions under the Bill of Rights, the idea is most clearly seen in cases where the Court does not and cannot plausibly relate its decision to any actual text.

Of these, the most notorious was the 1905 decision in *Lochner v. New York,* striking down a state law setting maximum hours for bakers to work. The Court had earlier invented an amorphous "right to contract," an individual liberty that is nowhere to be found in the Constitution itself. Justice Rufus Peckham, purporting to apply the 14th Amendment's Due Process Clause, said that statutes such as the one before the Court were "mere meddlesome interferences with the rights of the individual." However, it is now impolitic, indeed a major gaffe, to say so.

Peckham had a point—not a constitutional point but a philosophic one. He spoke for individual liberty in economic affairs, and there is no reason in terms of philosophy to prefer other freedoms to economic freedoms. If the Court insists upon deciding cases according to philosophy rather than law—which it should not do—then it should consider reviving *Lochner;* Judge Learned Hand put the point well: "I cannot help thinking that it would have seemed a strange anomaly to those who penned the words in the Fifth [Amendment] to learn that they constituted severer restrictions as to Liberty than Property. . . . I can see no more persuasive reason for supposing that a legislature is *a priori* less qualified to choose between 'personal' than between economic values; and there have been strong protests, to me unanswerable, that there is no constitutional basis for asserting a larger measure of judicial supervision over the first than over the second."

The distinction between personal and economic liberties is obviously false. Property does not claim liberty, people who own property do; contracts do not seek liberty, people who want to enter into agreements do. And those rights are every bit as "personal" as the right to abortion and homosexual sodomy, which the Court today upholds. There are moral and prudential differences that a legislature might choose to recognize, but the distinction between the two forms of liberty according to the arbitrary labels of "personal" and "economic" is irrational. It arises not from any constitutional argument but from the different moods and values of the dominant social classes of Peckham's time and ours.

The post-Civil War era was a period of robust economic expansion, and the class of businessmen and entrepreneurs, the elites of the time, set the values the Court protected. In our time, the dominant class consists of intellectuals (very broadly and loosely defined) and knowledge workers. Its members tend to look down on business and to elevate freedom of speech and personal morality over the economic freedoms required by a healthy economy. The Court may not follow the election returns, as Mr. Dooley claimed, but it follows, and reinforces, the values of the classes that enjoy social prestige. It is also noticeable that the modern Court strikes down laws with far greater frequency than did the Courts of the latter years of the 19th century and the first half of the 20th. The result is the much greater potency of what we may call intellectual class values. There appear to be several reasons for the increased intervention of the judiciary into our politics and practices of governance. The first is the Court's decision in the mid-20th century to begin incorporating the Bill of Rights, originally only a set of checks on the federal government, into the 14th Amendment, as guarantees of liberty against state governments. The occasions for constitutional scrutiny were thereby vastly multiplied. Second was the decision in *Brown v. Board of Education* (1954) outlawing segregation laws. The significance of that decision was that the Court believed it was accomplishing a great moral good without any justification in the Constitution, and it had prevailed over fierce opposition. I and others have argued that the decision could have been rooted in the Constitution, but the important point is that the Court did not think so and was thus encouraged to engage in further social reform with only lip service, if that, to the actual Constitution.

It quickly became apparent that further reform would consist of a move to the left. That is to say, it would involve centralization and the erosion of freedom in economic affairs and enormous permissiveness in social and moral matters. The Supreme Court fought a rearguard action to preserve federalism against New Deal economic legislation, provoking Franklin Roosevelt's Court-packing plan. That plan failed in Congress, largely because of Roosevelt's obvious disingenuousness: he presented the need for additional justices as a remedy for a Court grown old and unable to keep up with the demands of the work, when his transparent motive was to create a Court that would uphold New Deal legislation. Deaths and resignations shortly accomplished his goal in any event. Since then the Court has rarely interfered with economic regulations, no matter how irrational or implausibly related to acknowledged federal powers, such as the regulation of interstate commerce, taxation, and spending.

The idea of liberty as the Constitution—or rather, a majority of the Court—understands it moved to matters of individual choice in the personal and moral sphere. As Irving Kristol put it, the liberal ethos "aims simultaneously at political and social collectivism on the one hand, and moral anarchy on the other." We have seen that the Court willingly gave up the struggle against collectivism, including the economic variety. We will now turn to its encouragement of moral anarchy.

Moral anarchy is usually discussed as favoring liberty. It should not be. As such things as incessant vulgarity, obscenity and pornography, rap music celebrating the violent abuse of women and the killing of police proliferate, persons who want to live and raise families in a decent environment are deprived of a crucial liberty—one that they have tried to preserve through laws and regulation, only to find themselves overruled by courts entranced by the liberal ethos Kristol described. A few of the areas in which this is most clearly perceived are speech, religion, and sexuality.

The older idea of the speech protected by the First Amendment was stated by a *unanimous* Court in 1942 in *Chaplinsky v. New Hampshire*: there are certain well-defined and narrowly limited classes of speech, the prevention and punishment of which have never been thought to raise any Constitutional problem. These include the lewd and obscene, the profane, the libelous, and the insulting or "fighting" words—those that by their very utterance inflict injury or tend to incite an immediate breach of the peace. It has been well observed that such utterances are no essential part of any exposition of ideas, and are of such slight social value as a step to truth that any benefit that may be derived from them is clearly outweighed by the social interest in order and morality.

The liberty of the individual was thus subject to only minor restraints, but even those were soon abandoned. In *Cohen v. California* (1971), for example, the Court afforded First Amendment protection to a man who wore into a courthouse a jacket bearing the inspiring words "F . . . the Draft," saying "[O]ne man's vulgarity is another's lyric." Moral relativism thus became the essence of individual liberty as the Constitution understands it.

Cohen was no aberration. I wrote in 1990 that "It is unlikely, of course, that a general constitutional doctrine of the impermissibility of legislating moral standards will ever be framed." I was wrong. Case after case struck down convictions for, and thus validated, shouting obscenities in public places, the vilest pornography, even computer-simulated child pornography, which is becoming impossible to distinguish from live sex with children. The change in the understanding of free speech is demonstrated by the fact that in the early obscenity prosecutions, defendants' lawyers did not even bother to invoke the First Amendment. Now it is so routinely invoked that the Supreme Court was led to say that nude dancing, because it is "expressive," is entitled to considerable constitutional protection.

No other subject displays a greater divergence from the original constitutional understanding of individual liberty than that of religion. The modern Court has shown an unremitting hostility to public manifestations of religious belief. The idea that religion poses a unique danger lay behind the 1968 decision in *Flast v. Cohen*. It had been the universal rule that no one had standing to sue for an alleged constitutional violation merely by reason of being a citizen or taxpayer. Standing required that the litigant show concrete injury to himself. Dissatisfaction with governmental action would not suffice. That rule prevented the courts from becoming battlegrounds for abstract ideologies. In *Flast,* however, the plaintiff was granted standing as a taxpayer to challenge the expenditure of federal funds to aid religious schools. No other provision of the Constitution or its amendments can be enforced by a plaintiff alleging only that he is unhappy with a governmental action.

Not only have standing rules been abandoned in religious cases, but there has also been an almost unlimited expansion in the scope of the Establishment Clause of the First Amendment ("Congress shall make no law respecting an establishment of religion . . ."). The result has been a steady flow of cases (most often brought by the ACLU, which has an acute institutional allergy to religion, particularly to Christianity) outlawing crèches on public property, prayer in public schools, moments of silence before the start of the school day (some child might be praying undetected), the display of the Ten Commandments in a high school, a teacher reading the Bible in school during his free time, the recitation of a short nonsectarian prayer at a middle school commencement, etc. and etc.

Perhaps one reason for the constitutional objections to religion is that serious religions attempt to place restrictions on their members' behavior. Restrictions deriving from religious belief are, if not identical, at least first cousins to moral restraints imposed by law. In the eyes of the moral relativist, they are as objectionable as any moral imperative enforced by the state. For those who believe that individual liberty as the Constitution understands it is tantamount to moral relativism, therefore, religious restrictions must be ruled unconstitutional. In truth, however, there is absolutely no constitutional basis for the Court's anti-religion campaign. As scholarship, particularly Philip Hamburger's book *Separation of Church and State,* makes irrefutably clear, the Establishment Clause of the First Amendment means only that government may not establish an official church of the sort found in many European nations. Amusingly enough, when one justice pointed this out, another accused him of using an 18th century concept of establishment. Since the First Amendment was written, proposed, and ratified in the 18th century, the attempted refutation hardly seems germane, much less fatal to the point being made. The fact is that today there is not the remotest possibility of an establishment of religion anywhere in the United States, which means that the clause should be considered utterly obsolete, and certainly should not be used to launch attacks on ordinary and consensual religious practices that happen to take place in public.

A similar shift in individual liberty is observable in matters of sexuality. In *Poe v. Ullman* (1961), a case seeking to challenge Connecticut's ban on contraceptive use, Justice Harlan could write confidently that "Adultery, homosexuality, and the like are sexual intimacies which the State forbids." He contrasted these valid restrictions with efforts to regulate marital intimacies through the criminal law. When the statute came back before the Court in *Griswold v. Connecticut* (1965), Justice William O. Douglas's opinion relied heavily upon Harlan's rationale in creating a right of privacy for married couples. That right predictably expanded in later cases, first to cover anyone wishing to purchase and use contraceptives and then to other matters, including abortion.

But Harlan's dictum that acts such as adultery and homosexual sodomy could legitimately be proscribed seemed to hold. In *Bowers v. Hardwick* (1986) the Court by a majority of one upheld a law criminalizing homosexual sodomy, but it was Justice Harry Blackmun's dissent that forecast the shape of constitutional liberty to come. He first denied that the right of privacy invented in *Griswold* was confined to relations within the family: "We protect those rights not

72

because they contribute in some direct and material way, to the general public welfare, but because they form so central a part of an individual's life." Not satisfied with this extraordinary elevation of the individual above any claims of the family, Blackmun went on: "[T]he concept of privacy embodies the 'moral fact that a person belongs to himself and not others nor to society as a whole.'" This is to deny that society, much less kin, friends, or colleagues, have any valid claim upon the individual. That is a revolutionary, not to say sophomoric, notion of liberty.

The court's celebration of rampant individualism appears to have limits, at least for the time being. In *Washington v. Glucksburg* (1997), the justices refused to create a constitutional right to assisted suicide. This seems to fly in the face of cases such as *Eisenstadt v. Baird* (1972) where the Court upheld the right of persons, married or not, to purchase contraceptives because of the individual's right to be "free from unwarranted governmental intrusion into matters so fundamentally affecting a person as the decision whether to bear or beget a child." The Court in *Glucksburg* actually spoke of the sanctity of human life and the state's "unqualified interest in the preservation of human life." This, coming from a Court that finds a virtually unlimited right to abortion, seems, at the very least, ironic. It is not to be supposed that this continual evolution of the Constitution is entirely the work of the judiciary. Nor is it the work of the American public.

The evolution proceeds, after all, by invalidating laws and actions that are the work of the electorate's elected representatives. It is unmistakably the case that the Court's work sometimes follows and sometimes leads opinion trends in America's "elites"—university faculties, journalists, entertainers, foundation staffs, mainline churches, and governmental bureaucracies. These elites and the courts rely upon one another. The elites guide the judiciary and make the judges' decisions acceptable to the public, while the judiciary gives finality to elite opinion in a way that cannot be overturned by legislation. The aristocracy that the anti-Federalists feared has been created and empowered in large part by the very Bill of Rights they demanded as a bulwark against aristocracy.

There are heavy costs to this development. One is the decline of individual liberty as the Constitution originally understood it. The first freedom, implicit and taken for granted in the design of the Constitution, is the power of individuals to participate in making the laws by which they are governed. When an activist judiciary steadily creates rights it calls "constitutional" but which have no plausible roots in the historic Constitution, that liberty is just as steadily decreased. Justice Scalia put it well in a dissent: "What secret knowledge, one must wonder, is breathed into lawyers when they become Justices of this Court, that enables them to discern that a practice which the text of the Constitution does not clearly proscribe, and which our people have regarded as constitutional for 200 years, is in fact unconstitutional? . . . Day by day, case by case, [this Court] is busy designing a Constitution for a country I do not recognize."

Although it is not usually discussed in those terms, an activist Court also attacks the individual's interest in federalism and his nation's sovereignty. Ideas of morality and appropriate policies vary, sometimes drastically, by states and regions. Constitutional rulings often obliterate such differences and do so with flat rules about rights that leave no room for compromise and the normal processes of democracy. Citizens lose both their freedom to leave a jurisdiction whose policies they dislike and the political freedom to try to change those policies at the ballot box.

These were liberties the original Constitution assumed. Perhaps even further from the contemplation of the Founders is the recent inclination of a majority of the Court to create a trans-national Constitution by reliance on foreign judicial decisions, legislation, and even resolutions and treaties the United States has not adopted or ratified.

What are the prospects for individual liberty as the Constitution of the future will understand it? It is always perilous to predict the future by extrapolating from existing trends. On the other hand, the trends being discussed have persisted in virulent form for more than 60 years and there is little sign that they will halt or be reversed. The dominant social class is likely to remain the knowledge or intellectual class. Judges who belong to that class and find its assumptions congenial have become used to making policy regardless of the understanding of what they were doing by the men who made the Constitution law. National elections have not changed much. Justices appointed by Republicans vote in much the same way as those appointed by Democrats; the Court that gave us *Roe v. Wade* was comprised overwhelmingly of Republican appointees, and Republican justices have continued to reaffirm and to extend the rule of that case for more than 40 years.

As the example of *Roe* suggests, constitutional litigation and decisions can be highly divisive and harmful to our politics. Individual liberty will continue to diminish by increments as the judiciary takes more and more of the ability to govern from the hands of voters. One would have to be unconscious or supremely credulous not to see, for example, that the Court is chipping away at the death penalty with a view to its ultimate extinction, in defiance both of the Constitution and the voters of many states, and that its homosexual sodomy rulings were designed to lay the groundwork for a constitutional right to same sex marriage. The most pernicious aspect of this process is that the public is gradually led to believe that elite values are actually in the Constitution or to recognize that voters have no way of correcting the Court and so come docilely to accept the loss of their liberties.

The potential for more divisive and erroneous constitutional ruling in the future increases as America becomes an increasingly diverse society. Robert Putnam's study, confirming what even casual observation suggests, found that as diversity increases, the sense of community and trust decline. John Jay recognized the advantages of a fairly homogeneous society when he wrote in the second issue of *The Federalist*, "Providence has been pleased to give this one connected country to one united people—a people descended from the same ancestors, speaking the same language, professing the same religion, attached to the same principles of government, very similar in their manners and customs . . ." He went on to say that this country "should never be split into a number of unsocial, jealous, and alien sovereignties." Given America's diversity today—lacking the unifying traits that impressed Jay and increasingly split into a number of distrustful groups—can anyone imagine that our original Constitution could be written and ratified today? More than this, can anyone imagine that these groups will not seek to amend the Constitution by court rulings? Group rights are likely to trump many individual liberties. We have seen this already with affirmative action laws and procedures and court rulings that ratify them. Judge Learned Hand wrote in 1942: "[T]his much I think I do know—that a society so riven that the spirit of moderation is gone, no court *can* save; that a society where that spirit flourishes, no court *need* save; that in a society which evades its responsibility by thrusting on the courts the nurture of that spirit, that spirit in the end will perish." Moderation in our politics and the clamor for new rights is already diminishing our liberties. Group rights defined and enforced by courts are not a recipe for either individual liberty or social peace.

Nor are peace and liberty to be found in the modern elite values or in the judicial behavior that accepts them. For these elite values are deeply incoherent, as can be witnessed everywhere in the culture. Maureen Mullarkey notes the parallel in this respect between "conceptual art" and constitutional law: man is made for meaning, a communal achievement realized in concert with what used to be called natural law. Only when language is judged a product of arbitrary will rather than of cognition can it be "left to the viewer to construct meaning." The assent to intellectual anarchy, popularized in the arts, reached its apogee in *Planned Parenthood* v. *Casey*'s famous defense of individualized deduction: "At the heart of liberty is the right to define one's own concept of existence, of meaning, of the universe, and the mystery of human life."

Only the mad, quarantined by unshared, idiosyncratic conceptions of reality, suffer that kind of freedom. The privatization of meaning signals something larger than an art-world posture. Antirational, it thwarts the basis for making the distinctions on which decisions, aesthetic and moral, rest. Mullarkey also remarks on "the resentment of rationality and of socially embraced patterns of meaning." Individual liberty will not find a secure home in a world where this resentment prevails.

What the original Constitution and Bill of Rights had to say about individual liberty is a far cry from what the judicially amended Constitution has to say and will say in the future. When considering the prospects for liberty, we should bear in mind that absolute authority, a disdain for the historic Constitution, and philosophic incompetence are a lethal combination. The only solution apparent would appear to be the political defeat of our current elites accompanied by a defection of some members of the elites from their present monolithic attitudes. That may seem a utopian fantasy, but changes in the culture and the reading of the Constitution have occurred in the past. Although these changes have proved largely deleterious, they demonstrate that change is not only possible but also inevitable. Unless we assume that the culture war is irretrievably lost, and with it an increasing number of our liberties, our responsibility is to return our constitutional understanding as closely as possible to the first principles of the Founders' plan.

Academic Freedom
and What It Means Today

Robert P. George

At the heart of Western ideas of liberty is the freedom to pursue rational inquiry wherever it may lead. This freedom, won against opposition from sovereigns, ecclesiastics, and the censors of the modern state, is among the most precious legacies of the Enlightenment. Robert P. George, professor of politics at Princeton University, and founder of the Madison Program in American Institutions, explores the growing threat of academic censorship as the liberal orthodoxy responds to the presence on campus of people who do not conform to it.

When the flower children and anti-war activists of the 1960s came to power in the universities, they did not overthrow the idea of liberal arts education. In a great many cases, they proclaimed themselves true partisans of liberal arts ideals. True, many influential representatives of that generation believe that universities should be producing leftwing social activists, with more than a few eager to transform university education into a species of vocational training for aspiring ACLU lawyers, Planned Parenthood volunteers, and Barack Obama-style "community organizers." There are even colleges and universities that offer academic credit for social activism. Others, however, resist the idea that learning should be instrumentalized in this way. They profess allegiance to the traditional (or, in any event, traditional-sounding) idea that the point of liberal education is to enrich and liberate the student. That is what is supposed to be "liberal" about liberal arts learning—that it conveys the knowledge, skills, and habits of mind that carry with them a certain profound form of freedom.

However traditional this may *sound*, there is nevertheless an unbridgeable chasm between the idea of liberal arts education as classically conceived and the conception sponsored and promoted by some (though, mercifully, not all) in authority in the academy today. Many academic humanists and social scientists propose *liberation* as the goal of liberal arts learning, to be sure. But the question is, liberation from *what*?

In their conception (what I shall call the revisionist conception), it is liberation from traditional social constraints and norms of morality—from the beliefs, principles, and structures by which earlier generations had been taught to govern their conduct for the sake of personal virtue and the common good.

Why do they regard this form of "liberation" as desirable? Because it has become a matter of dogma that the traditional norms and structures are irrational—vestiges of superstition and phobia that impede the free development of personalities by restricting people's capacities to act on their desires.

In this dogmatic context, the purpose of liberal arts learning is to undermine whatever is left of the old norms and structures. To accomplish the task, teaching and scholarship are meant either (1) to expose the texts and traditions once regarded as the intellectual treasures of our civilization—the Bible, Plato, Dante, Aquinas, Chaucer, Shakespeare, Austen, Locke, Gibbon, the authors of *The Federalist*, etc.—as mere works of propaganda on behalf of unjust (racist, sexist, classist, homophobic, etc.) social orders, or yet more insidiously (2) to show how the old texts and traditions can be "reappropriated" and used as tools to subvert the modern forms of social injustice.

And beyond this, liberal arts learning is meant to enable students to become truly "authentic" individuals—people who are true to themselves. But what is the "self" to which the authentic person is true? For those in the grip of the new liberationist ideology, to be true to one's *self* is to act on one's *desires*. Indeed, people are defined by their desires. Authenticity consists in doing what you really want to do, in defiance, if necessary, of expectations based on putatively outmoded moral ideas and social norms.

According to this conception, whatever impedes you from doing what you truly want to do (unless, that is, what you want to do is in violation of some norm of political correctness) is a mere hang-up—something that holds you back from being the person you truly are. Such impediments, be they religious convictions, moral ideals, or what have you, are to be transcended for the sake of the free and full development of your personality. The essence of liberation is transcending such hang-ups, for example, by "coming out" as a homosexual, transvestite, polyamorist, or a member of some other "sexual minority" and acting on sexual desires that might have been "repressed" as a result of religious and moral convictions.

Nowhere is this clearer than in Freshman orientation programs that feature compulsory events calculated to undermine any lingering traditional beliefs about sexual morality. These events are advertised by university officials as efforts to discourage date rape, unwanted pregnancy, sexually transmitted diseases, bullying, and so forth. Because they are designed precisely to establish and reinforce campus orthodoxies, however, they are invariably exercises in liberationist propaganda. Dissenting views, such as the view that sodomy and promiscuity are immoral and affronts to human dignity, are never aired. The manifest point is to send the clearest possible message to students who may dissent from the liberationist orthodoxy that they are outsiders who had better conform or keep their mouths shut.

A young friend of mine who attended prestigious Williams College tells a story that could be told by students and recent alumni of similar institutions, from Bates to Pomona. Shortly after arriving at the college, the new students were divided into small groups to discuss campus life. Each group was led by an official moderator. Attendance was mandatory. The moderator informed the students that it was important for each of them to understand sympathetically what it was like to come out as "gay." The presupposition, of course, was that a person who experiences strong or dominant homosexual inclinations or desires *must* come out as "gay" in order to be true to himself. No alternative view was presented, despite the fact that belief in sexual restraint and traditional sexual morality generally, not to mention reticence concerning one's personal feelings pertaining to sex, is by no means a monopoly held by "straights."

The moderator's next move was to direct each student to state his or her name and say, "I am gay." So around the table they went, with students, all too predictably, conforming to the moderator's absurd and offensive directive. "I'm Sarah Smith, and I am gay." "I'm Seth Farber, and I am gay." When it was my friend's turn, he politely but firmly refused. The moderator, of course, demanded an explanation. With some trepidation he replied by simply stating the truth: "This exercise is absurd and offensive and has nothing to do with the purposes for which I and others came to Williams College, namely, to learn to think carefully, critically, and *for ourselves.*" Confirming the old dictum that bullies are cowards who will never stand up to people who have the temerity to stand up to them, the moderator backed off.

Now, of course, what goes on in these collegiate re-education camps is *radically* different from the classical understanding of what liberal arts education is supposed to accomplish. *Formally*, the classical and the revisionist conceptions are similar. Both propose the liberal arts as *liberating*. Both promise to enable the student to achieve a greater measure of *personal authenticity*. But in substance they could not be farther apart. They are polar opposites. The classical understanding of the goal of liberal arts learning is not to liberate us to act on our desires, but rather, and precisely, *to liberate us from slavery to them*. Personal authenticity, under the traditional account, consists in *self-mastery*—placing reason in control of desire.

According to the classical liberal arts ideal, learning promises liberation, but it is not liberation from demanding moral ideals and social norms—it is, rather, liberation from *slavery to self*. How can it be liberating to enter into the great conversation with Plato and his interlocutors? Why does the study of Augustine, Dante, or Aquinas help us to be free? Beyond being entertained by Shakespeare's charm, wit, and astonishing intellectual deftness, why should we make the effort to understand and appreciate the plays and sonnets? According to the classical liberal arts ideal, our critical engagement with great thinkers enriches our understanding and enables us to grasp, or grasp more fully, great truths—truths that, when we appropriate them and integrate them into our lives, liberate us from what is merely vulgar, coarse, or base. These are soul-shaping, humanizing truths—truths whose appreciation and secure possession elevate reason above passion or appetite, enabling us to direct our desires and our wills to what is truly good, truly beautiful, truly worthy of human beings as possessors of a profound and inherent dignity. The classical liberal arts proposition is that intellectual knowledge has a role to play in making self-transcendence possible. It can help us to understand what is good and to love the good above whatever it is we happen to desire, and it can teach us to desire what is good because it is good, thus making us truly *masters of ourselves*.

These contrasting views of liberal learning reflect competing understandings of what human beings fundamentally are and what is possible for us to be or become. I have spoken of the soul-shaping power of truths, but on the revisionist view there neither is nor can be any such thing as a rational soul. There is merely a "self." And the "self" is constituted not by powers of rationality that enable us to know what is humanly good and morally right and direct our desires toward it but, rather, by our desires themselves.

Reason's role in our conduct can be nothing more than instrumental. It is not, and cannot be, the master of desire, but only its servant. Reason cannot tell us what to want, but only how to obtain whatever it is we happen to want. As David Hume articulated the point, "Reason is and ought only to be the slave of the passions, and may pretend to no office other than to serve and obey them." In this view, the rational soul is an illusion, and belief in it and in truths that can liberate us from slavery to our desires is something not unlike a superstition. Human fulfillment consists not in overcoming desires that run contrary to what reason identifies as good and right but, rather, in freeing ourselves from "irrational" inhibitions (those "hang-ups") that impede us from doing as we please. Hence the slogan that will ever stand as a sort of verbal monument to the Me Generation: "If it feels good, do it."

The true liberal arts ideal rejects the reduction of reason to the status of passion's slave. It is an ideal rooted in the conviction that there are human goods and a common good, in light of which we have *reasons* to constrain, to limit, to regulate, and even to alter our desires. It proposes the study of great works with a view to grasping more fully these goods and the reasons they provide, and to understanding them in their wholeness. What liberal arts learning offers us is a truly audacious hope, the hope of self-mastery. Can it really be true? What could there be in us, or about us, that could actually make it possible for human beings to be masters of their desires, feelings, emotions, and passions and not mere slaves to them? Only this mysterious thing that Plato's Socrates was so concerned about, and about which so many great thinkers and writers of the Western intellectual tradition from Plato forward have sought to understand and teach us: the soul. Soulless "selves" could have desires and even a certain form of purely instrumental rationality directed toward achieving their efficient satisfaction, but soulless "selves" could never be masters of their desires. Only by virtue of our rational souls can we exercise the more than instrumental forms of rationality that free us from the chains of appetite.

Now, if you believe that reason is not the slave of the passions but is capable of mastering them, then you must acknowledge the existence of human *virtues*—the dispositions that enable reason to prevail over impulse whenever the two conflict. You must believe that there are qualities that make for an honorable, worthy, upright life, habits and traits of character that we should cultivate in ourselves so as not to be governed by our impulses but self-directed toward the good. A few years ago, the wonderful documentary filmmaker Michael Pack and the no less wonderful historian-biographer Richard Brookhiser visited us at Princeton to offer an advance viewing of their film biography, *Rediscovering George Washington*. Some of the students were perplexed when Brookhiser explained to them that Washington came to be who he was by imagining an ideal, truly noble individual. As a young man, the future statesman formed a picture of the kind of person he would like to be and then tried to become that person by acting the way that person would act. He "stepped into the role" he had designed for himself. He sought to make himself virtuous by ridding himself of wayward desires or passions that would have no place in the character and life of the noble individual he sought to emulate and, by emulating, to become.

Now, for someone who understands and believes in the classical liberal arts idea and its ideal of self-mastery, there is nothing in the least inauthentic about Washington's imagining what a virtuous person would be like and then trying to become such a person by living out the virtues he would embody. On the contrary, this is an act of the most profound authenticity. Washington sought to be master of himself rather than a slave to his desires. But to some of the students, Washington's conduct seemed *radically* inauthentic. He was play-acting, they protested; he wasn't really being himself. He was trying to live a life that wasn't his own, because he wasn't affirming and following his desires; rather, he was trying to reshape his desires in line with standards drawn, as one of them put it, from "outside himself."

Not all the students saw things this way, but we can explain why some of them did. They had absorbed the revisionist notion of what a person is. Influenced by the prevailing orthodoxies, they had come to see the person as a soulless self, governed by desires, whose liberation consists in freeing those desires from constraints, be they formal or informal, external or internal. They had not so much as considered the alternative view of man that is at the core of the classical conception of the liberal arts, namely, the view of man as a rational creature capable of self-transcendence and self-mastery. Why had they not considered it? Because it had never been presented to them as an option *worth* considering.

The true founder of the liberal arts ideal was Socrates as presented by his student Plato. And Socrates's method of teaching was to question. He is the great exemplar of what the late Allan Bloom labeled "the interrogatory attitude." The liberal arts ideal assumes, to be sure, that there are right answers to great moral and existential questions. It is the enemy, not the friend, of moral relativism. But liberal arts teaching is not fundamentally about telling students what the right answers are—even when we are justifiably confident that we have the right answers. Nor is liberal arts learning merely a matter of receiving and processing information, even if it's great information, such as historical facts about the Western tradition or the American founding. Nor is it merely a matter of reading Aristotle, or Chaucer, or Shakespeare, or Tocqueville and knowing what these great writers said. Liberal arts education is about *engaging* with these things, wrestling with them and the questions they suggest. It is about considering arguments and counter-arguments, examining competing points of view.

And the range of competing alternatives students should be invited to consider, while not limitless, needs to be wide. Liberal arts education is not a catechism class. Students should not simply be presented with officially approved views—even if they are the right views. I want my own students to consider seriously a range of possibilities, including some—Marxism, for example—that I think are not only unsound but also reprehensible, and whose record in human affairs is a record of death and abomination. I certainly want them to hear the profound arguments advanced against Marxism by people like Hayek, Solzhenitsyn, and John Paul II. But I also want them to understand how it was that Marxism could have attracted the allegiance of many intelligent and morally serious (if seriously misguided) people. I want them to know the arguments Marx and his most intelligent disciples made. In fact, I want them to consider these arguments fairly on their merits. The task of the liberal arts teacher, as I envisage it, is not to tell students what to think; it is to teach them to think, as my young friend said, carefully, critically, and for themselves. Now *why*? Is it because I think there is something *intrinsically* valuable about the interrogatory attitude? Allan Bloom might have thought so. The possibility that he did is what opened him to the charge of relativism and even nihilism advanced by some culturally conservative critics of Bloom's influential book *The Closing of the American Mind*. Walker Percy, for example, faulted Bloom for allegedly holding the view that the point of an open mind is merely to have an open mind, rather than to arrive at answers that are to be affirmed and acted on.

Whether or not the charge is just, the charge, if true, would be damning. The idea of a mind that never closes on a truth is antithetical to the liberal arts ideal. The point of the interrogatory attitude, rather, is precisely to move from ignorance to truths—truths that can be affirmed and acted on. As G.K. Chesterton once said, the point of an open mind is like the point of an open mouth: to close on something solid.

We begin to understand the much misunderstood and abused concept of academic freedom when we consider the central importance of the interrogative attitude to the enterprise of liberal arts learning. The interrogative attitude will flourish only under conditions of freedom. It can be smothered by speech codes and the like, to be sure, but it can be smothered in less obvious ways. It can be smothered when well-qualified scholars, teachers, and academic administrators are denied positions in institutions that claim to be nonpartisan and nonsectarian, or when they are denied tenure or promotion or are subjected to discriminatory treatment for dissenting from campus orthodoxies. It can be smothered by an atmosphere of political correctness, which may, of course, be conservative but in most places today is a phenomenon of the left. It can fail to emerge wherever teaching and learning are governed by orthodoxies that refuse to subject themselves to questioning.

Crystal Dixon was the associate vice president of human resources at the University of Toledo. She is an African American woman and a faithful Christian. In April 2008, she wrote a letter to the editor of her local newspaper, rejecting the claim that "sexual orientation," as it has ambiguously come to be called, is like race and should be included alongside race, ethnicity, sex, and the like as a category in antidiscrimination and civil rights laws. When her letter was published, the president of the University of Toledo, a man named Lloyd Jacobs, suspended her from her job and threatened further punishment if she did not recant and apologize for publishing a view that he evidently regards as heretical. What is remarkable about this case is how unremarkable it is. Scarcely a week passes without some offense being committed by a university or its administrators or faculty against intellectual or academic freedom. Given the strong leftward tilt and the manifest ideological imbalance at most of our nation's colleges and universities, it is almost always the case that the victim of the attack is a student, professor, or member of the administrative staff who has dared to write or say something (whether in a classroom, a publication, or a casual conversation) that disputes a left-wing dogma, such as the belief that there is nothing morally wrong or even questionable about homosexual conduct and that "sexual orientation" is akin to race.

Whatever his other troubles and vulnerabilities at the time, it is worth remembering that what triggered the fall of Larry Summers as president of Harvard was his merely raising an intellectual question about whether disparities between men and women in scientific achievement might have something to do with nature as well as nurture. Previous successes at enforcing political correctness made it possible to bring down even someone as powerful as a president of Harvard for asking a politically incorrect question. Summers's fall, in turn, strengthened the hand of those who wish to rule out of bounds the questioning of campus orthodoxies. And it sent a chill wind through the academy. After all, if the president of Harvard can be brought down for a thought crime, what public dissenter from the prevailing dogmas can be safe?

Yet all is not darkness. Earlier this year, the department of sociology at the University of Virginia voted against granting tenure to an outstanding young scholar of family sociology named Bradford Wilcox. Despite his extraordinary record of intellectual achievement and distinguished teaching, Professor Wilcox was punished for his conservative religious and moral opinions—opinions that his politically correct opponents were foolish enough to mention freely in discussions prior to the vote on his application for tenure. Although Wilcox's tenure denial was initially upheld by university administrators, the university's president, John T. Casteen, reviewed the case and reversed the decision. Wilcox has been granted tenure. By rectifying a gross and manifest injustice, President Casteen struck an important blow for academic freedom and with it a blow for the interrogative attitude and the liberal arts ideal—one that will send a message not only to his own faculty at the University of Virginia but also to students and faculties at institutions around the country.

It is the Larry Summers episode at Harvard in reverse: it will give courage to those who dissent from prevailing opinions and help them to stand up and say what they actually think, and it will serve as a warning to those who would attempt to punish them. The warning is that those who abuse the power of their offices by trying to punish dissenters will lose out—and their loss will expose them as enemies of free intellectual inquiry, in other words, people who themselves have no place in a university.

As we consider the disgraceful behavior of one university president in Crystal Dixon's case and the encouraging conduct of another in the case of Bradford Wilcox, perhaps it is worth pausing to ask why we care—or should care—so much about intellectual freedom in the academy. Why ought we to be concerned about the rights of an administrator who is suspended for stating her moral views or the freedom of an assistant professor who is denied tenure because he would not toe the party line? Why should we care as much as we do about students who are punished with a bad grade for having the temerity to state views that are out of line with those of the course instructor? What is it about intellectual freedom that makes it worth worrying about—and worth fighting for?

In my view, it is not—or not merely—a passion for freedom for its own sake. We want our young people and those responsible for teaching them to be free from repression or invidious discrimination, but we should fight for these freedoms for a reason that goes significantly beyond them. We should fight for freedom *from* oppression on our campuses because we believe that academic freedom is freedom *for* something—something profoundly important, namely, the intellectual excellence that makes self-mastery possible. We want students and scholars to be able to pursue understanding, knowledge, and truth more robustly and to appropriate the great goods of human intellectual striving more fully into their lives. We should honor academic freedom as a great and indispensable value because it serves other values—understanding, knowledge, and truth—that are greater still.

Although some have depicted freedom and truth as antithetical, in reality they are mutually supportive and, indeed, dependent on each other. Any plausible and complete case for academic freedom will show it to be an essential means to knowledge. It is because we value truth that we value the freedom that enables us to discover it. The overwhelming evidence of history, not to mention the plain evidence under our noses from the contemporary situation, shows that freedom is as necessary to the intellectual life of man as oxygen is to his bodily life.

Should academic freedom be boundless? Of course not. But the scope of freedom must be generous—especially in the academy, where free inquiry, exploration, and experimentation are the primary purpose. Even within its legitimate bounds, can academic freedom not be abused? Of course it can be, and is. Academic freedom does not guarantee excellence (or even passable scholarship or teaching). Sometimes respect for it insulates abuses from correction. But, again, the lessons of history and of our current situation are clear: repression of academic freedom—far from shielding us from error—undermines the process whereby errors are detected.

But someone might say: "There are many truths we know. Why must we permit them to be denied and questioned? Why not take the view that error—or at least clear error—has no rights? Otherwise, doesn't the defense of academic freedom collapse into the self-stultifying denial of the possibility of truth? Doesn't it make freedom, rather than truth, the ultimate academic value?" In response to such worries I would argue that the possibility of error is not the primary or most powerful reason for honoring academic freedom—or protecting it even in areas where we are secure in our knowledge of the truth. The stronger and deeper reason is that freedom is the condition of our fuller *appropriation* of the truth. I use this term because knowledge and truth have their value for human beings precisely as fulfillment of capacities for understanding and judgment. The liberal arts are *liberating* of the human spirit because knowledge of truth—attained by the exercise of our rational faculties—is *intrinsically* and not merely instrumentally valuable.

"Useful knowledge" is, of course, all to the good, and it is wonderful when human knowledge can serve other human goods, such as health, as in the biomedical sciences, or economic efficiency and growth, or the constructing of great buildings and bridges, or any of a million other worthy purposes.

But even "useful knowledge" is often more than merely instrumentally valuable, and a great deal of knowledge that wouldn't qualify as "useful" in the instrumental sense is intrinsically and profoundly enriching *and liberating*. This is why we honor—and should honor more highly than we currently do in our institutions of higher learning—academic excellence, whether in the humanities or the sciences. Knowledge that elevates and enriches—knowledge that liberates the human spirit—cannot be merely notional. *It must be appropriated.* It is not—*it cannot be*—merely a matter of affirming or even believing correct propositions. The knowledge that elevates and liberates is knowledge not only *that* something is the case, but why and how it is the case. And typically such knowledge does more than merely settle something in one's mind; it opens new avenues of exploration. Its payoff includes new sets of questions, new lines of inquiry, and the affirmation of the intellectual life.

To return, then, to the question: why respect freedom even where truth is known securely? I answer in the tradition of Socrates and, as Michael Novak would remind us, also the Second Vatican Council of the Catholic Church in its great Declaration on Religious Freedom: it is because freedom—freedom to inquire, freedom to assent or withhold assent as one's best judgment dictates—is a condition of the personal appropriation of the truth by the human subject. Knowledge of truth is intrinsically valuable not in some free-floating or abstract sense but precisely as an aspect of the well-being and fulfillment of human beings—rational creatures whose flourishing consists in part in intellectual inquiry, understanding, and judgment and in the practice of the virtues that make these possible. The freedom we must defend is freedom for the practice of these virtues. It is freedom for excellence, the freedom that enables us to master ourselves. It is a freedom that, far from being negated by rigorous standards of scholarship, demands them. It is not the freedom of "if it feels good, do it"; it is, rather, the freedom of self-transcendence, the freedom from slavery to self.

Feminism and Freedom

Christina Sommers

Feminism has become a powerful presence in Western societies, often taking a radical form, devoted to the extirpation of "patriarchy" and the curtailing of the power and the freedom of men. The history of the women's movement has been distorted by the radical feminists. So argues the distinguished writer and philosopher Christina Sommers in her defense of another kind of feminism, one in which traditional feminine values, such as marriage, family, and home, achieve the recognition that the real leaders of the women's movement in fact accorded to them.

On February 10, 2001, 18,000 women filled Madison Square Garden for one of the more notable feminist gatherings of our time. The event—"Take Back the Garden"—centered on a performance of Eve Ensler's raunchy play, *The Vagina Monologues*. The "Vulva Choir" sang; self-described "Vagina Warriors"—including Gloria Steinem, Jane Fonda, and Donna Hanover (Rudolph Giuliani's ex-wife)—recited pet names for their vaginas: Mimi, Gladys. Glenn Close led the crowd in spelling out the obscene word for women's intimate anatomy, "Give me a C. . . !!!" A huge banner declared the Garden to be a "RAPE FREE ZONE." The mood grew solemn when

Oprah Winfrey came forward to read a new monologue called "Under the Burqa," which described the plight of Afghan women living under the Taliban. At its climax, an actual Afghan woman named Zoya, who represented RAWA—the Revolutionary Association of the Women of Afghanistan—appeared on stage covered from head to toe in a burqa. Oprah approached her and, with a dramatic sweep of her arm, lifted and removed it. The crowd roared in delight.

Later, an exposé in the progressive *American Prospect* would reveal that RAWA is a Maoist organization whose fanatical members are so feared by Afghan women that one human rights activist has dubbed them the "Talibabes." According to the *Prospect*, when *Ms.* magazine tried to distance itself from RAWA in 2002, a RAWA spokeswoman denounced *Ms.* as "the "mouthpiece of hegemonic, U.S-centric corporate feminism." But on that magical February night at the Garden, few knew or cared about Zoya's political views or affiliations.

The evening was a near-perfect distillation of "contemporary feminism." Pick up a women's studies textbook, visit a college women's center, or look at the websites of leading feminist organizations and you will be likely to find the same fixation on intimate anatomy combined with left-wing politics and a poisonous antipathy to men. (Campus feminists were among the most vocal and zealous accusers of the young men on the Duke University lacrosse team, who were falsely indicted for rape in 2006.) Contemporary feminism routinely depicts American society as a dangerous patriarchy where women are under siege. That is the message of the "RAPE FREE ZONE" banner in the Garden. It therefore presents itself as a movement of "liberation," defying the patriarchal oppressor and offering women everywhere the opportunity to make contact with their "real selves."

But modern "women's liberation" has little to do with liberty. It aims not to free women to pursue their own interests and inclinations, but rather to re-educate them to attitudes often profoundly contrary to their natures. In *Professing Feminism: Education and Indoctrination in Women's Studies* (2003), two once-committed women's studies professors, Daphne Patai and Noretta Koertge, describe how the feminist classroom transforms idealistic female students into "relentless grievance collectors." In 1991, the culture critic and dissident feminist Camille Paglia put the matter even more bluntly: she described women's studies as "a jumble of vulgarians, bunglers, whiners, French faddicts, apparatchiks, dough-faced party-liners, pie-in-the-sky utopians and bullying sanctimonious sermonizers. Reasonable, moderate feminists hang back and keep silent in the face of fascism."

The embarrassing spectacle at Madison Square Garden, the erratic state of women's studies, the outbreak of feminist vigilantism at Duke University may tempt some to conclude that the women's movement in the United States is in a state of hopeless, hapless, and permanent disarray. Perhaps American feminism has become hysterical because it has ceased to be useful. After all, women in this country have their freedom; they have achieved parity with men in most of the ways that count. Why not let the feminist movement fade from the scene? The sooner the better. Good riddance.

That is an understandable but unwarranted reaction. We should not forget that women's emancipation is a critical chapter in the history of liberty. And, for most of the world's women, that story has just begun. Classical feminism offers to those women who have yet to obtain them a tried and true roadmap to equality and freedom. Moreover, even in the West there are unresolved equity issues, and the work of feminism is not over. Who needs feminism? We do. The world does. Women everywhere need the liberty to be what they are. What the contemporary feminist movement in America advocates, however, is a liberation *from* what they are. This we can see if we look back at the history of the women's movement, not as it is taught in women's studies departments, but as it truly was.

The classical feminism of the 18th and 19th centuries embodied two distinct schools of thought and social activism. The first, egalitarian feminism, was progressive (in the view of many contemporaries of both sexes, radical), and it centered on women as independent agents rather than wives and mothers. It held that men and women are, in their essential nature, the same, and it sought to liberate women through abstract appeals to social justice and universal rights. The second school, conservative feminism, was traditionalist and family-centered. It embraced rather than rejected women's established roles as homemakers, caregivers, and providers of domestic tranquillity—and it promoted women's rights by redefining, strengthening, and expanding those roles. Conservative feminists argued that a practical, responsible femininity could be a force for good in the world beyond the family, through charitable works and more enlightened politics and government.

Of the two schools, conservative feminism was much the more influential. Unlike its more radical sister, conservative feminism has always had great appeal to large majorities of women. By contrast, egalitarian feminists often appeared strange and frightening with their salons and little journals. It is not, however, my purpose to denigrate egalitarian feminism—quite the contrary. Historically, proponents of the two schools were forthright and sometimes fierce competitors, but their competition sharpened the arguments on both sides, and they often cooperated on practical causes to great effect. The two movements were (and will remain) rivals in principle but complementary in practice. Thanks to egalitarian feminism, women now have the same rights and opportunities as men. And, as conservative feminists have always insisted, free women seldom aspire to be just like men but, rather, employ their freedom in distinctive ways and for distinctive purposes.

Egalitarian feminism had its historical beginnings in the writings of the British philosopher Mary Wollstonecraft (1759–1797). Wollstonecraft, a rebel and a free thinker, believed that women were as intelligent as men and as worthy of respect. Her *A Vindication of the Rights of Woman* became an instant sensation. She wrote it in the spirit of the European Enlightenment, whose primary principle was the essential dignity and moral equality of all rational beings. However, Wollstonecraft's insistence that women too are rational and deserving of the same rights as men was then a contentious thesis.

Wollstonecraft's demand was a dramatic break with the past. In 1776, Abigail Adams famously wrote a letter to her husband, John, urging him and his colleagues in the Continental Congress to "remember the ladies . . . and to be more generous and favorable to them than your ancestors." Adams was appealing to a tradition of chivalry and gallantry that enjoined male protectiveness toward women. Sixteen years later, in her *Vindication*, Wollstonecraft was doing something markedly different. She was not urging legislators in France and England to "remember the ladies" or appealing to their generous or protective impulses. Reason, she said, demanded that women be granted the same rights as men. She wanted nothing less than total political and moral equality. Wollstonecraft was perhaps the first woman in history to insist that biology is not destiny: "I view with indignation the mistaken notions that enslave my sex."

For Wollstonecraft, education was the key to female liberation: "Strengthen the female mind by enlarging it, and there will be an end to blind obedience." She was a proponent of co-education and insisted that women be educated on a par with men—with all fields and disciplines being open to them. In the opening lines of *Vindication*, she expresses her "profound conviction that the neglected education of [women] is the grand source of the misery I deplore."

Wollstonecraft led one of the most daring, dramatic, and consequential lives of the 18th century. She was a lower-middle-class, semi-educated "nobody" (as one British historian has described her) who was to become the first woman to enter the Western canon of political philosophy. Her friends included Thomas Paine, William Wordsworth, and William Blake. She carried on a famous debate with Edmund Burke about the merits of the French Revolution. Soon after she published her *Vindication of the Rights of Woman* she ran off to Paris to write about the revolution.

After her death, her husband William Godwin wrote what he thought was an adulatory biography. He talked honestly about her unorthodox lifestyle, which included love affairs, an out-of wedlock child, and two suicide attempts over her faithless American lover. He even praised her—completely inaccurately—for having rejected Christianity. Godwin all but destroyed her reputation for the next hundred years. The public reaction to his disclosures was fascination, horror, and repulsion. Former friends denounced her. Feminists distanced themselves. Political enemies called her a "whore." Today, however, her reputation is secure. In an essay published in 1932, Virginia Woolf wrote, "One form of immortality is hers undoubtedly: she is alive and active, she argues and experiments, we hear her voice and trace her influence even now among the living." Woolf summarizes Wollstonecraft's egalitarian teachings in one sentence. "The staple of her doctrine was that nothing matters save independence." Another way of putting it is to say that what Wollstonecraft wanted for women was the full liberty of citizenship.

At the time Wollstonecraft was writing, the redoubtable Hannah More (1745–1833) and her Bluestocking allies were waging an equally consequential campaign to improve the status of women. More is well known to scholars who specialize in 18th-century culture. The late UCLA literary historian Mitzi Myers calls More a "female crusader infinitely more successful than Wollstonecraft or any other competitor." But More is rarely given the credit she deserves for her crusade. The story of what More initiated and how she did it is integral to the story of women's quest for freedom. But most feminists of the Second Wave have not wanted that story to be told.

Virginia Woolf once said that if she were in charge of assigning names to critical historical epochs, along with the Crusades or the War of the Roses she would give a special name to that world-transforming period at the end of the 18th century in England, when, in her words, "The middleclass woman began to write." One disparaging historian called this unprecedented cohort of writing women (borrowing a phrase from the 16th-century religious Reformer John Knox) "a monstrous regiment." It was a regiment that was destined to win decisive battles in women's struggle for freedom and opportunity. Its three most important members were Mary Wollstonecraft, Jane Austen, and Hannah More.

More was a novelist, poet, pamphleteer, political activist, evangelical reformer, and abolitionist. Some historians credit her political writings with saving England from the kind of brutal revolutionary upheaval that traumatized France. She was a close friend of Samuel Johnson and Horace Walpole, and an indispensable ally and confidante to William Wilberforce, the father of British abolitionism. She was surely the most prominent woman of her day. As one biographer notes, "In her time she was better known than Mary Wollstonecraft and her books outsold Jane Austen's many times over." Her various pamphlets sold in the millions, and her tract against the French Revolution enjoyed a greater circulation than Burke's *Reflections* or Paine's *Rights of Man*.

More (who never married) was active in the Bluestocking society. The "Blues" were a group of intellectual women (and men) who would meet to discuss politics, literature, science, and philosophy. The group was started in 1750 by intelligent but education-starved upper- and middle-class women who yearned for serious conversation rather than the customary chatter and gossip typical of elite gatherings. "I was educated at random," More would say, and women's education became one of her most passionate causes.

More is hard to classify politically: it is possible to find passages in her novels, pamphlets, and letters that make her look like an arch conservative, others that show her to be a progressive reformer. Through selective citation she can be made to seem like an insufferable prude—Lord Byron dismissed her as "Morality's prim personification"—but it is doubtful that a "prim personification" would have attracted the devotion and respect of men like Johnson, Walpole, and Wilberforce.

More was a British patriot, a champion of constitutional monarchy, and a friend and admirer of Edmund Burke. But she was no defender of the status quo. She called for revolutionary change—not in politics but in morals. In her novels and pamphlets, she sharply reproached members of the upper classes for their amorality, hedonism, indifference to the poor, and tolerance of the crime of slavery. In the many Sunday schools she established she encouraged the poor to be sober, thrifty, hard-working, and religious. More shared Adam Smith's enthusiasm for the free market as a force for good. But for the market to thrive, she believed England's poor and rich would need to develop good moral habits and virtuous characters.

Historians who are not ill-disposed toward More have called her a "bourgeois progressivist," a "Christian capitalist," "Burke for beginners," the "first Victorian." She could also be called the first conservative feminist. Unlike Wollstonecraft, More believed the sexes were significantly different in their propensities, aptitudes, and life preferences. But she envisioned a society where women's characteristic virtues and graces could be developed, refined, and freely expressed. She was persuaded that these virtues could be realized only when women were given more freedom and a serious education:

> Till women shall be more reasonably educated, and until the native growth of their mind shall cease to be more stilted and cramped, we shall have no juster ground for pronouncing that their understanding has already reached its highest attainable perfection, than the Chinese would have for affirming that their women have attained to the greatest possible perfection in walking, while their first care is, during their infancy, to cripple their feet.

More loathed the mindless pastimes that absorbed upper-class women of her day, and she encouraged middle- and upper-class women to leave their homes and salons so as to take up serious philanthropic pursuits. According to More, women were more tender-minded than men and were the natural caretakers of the nation. She told women that it was their patriotic duty to apply their natural gifts—nurturing, organizing, and educating—not merely to their own households but to society at large. "Charity," said one of More's fictional characters, "is the calling of a lady; the care of the poor is her profession." More envisioned armies of intelligent, informed, and well-trained women working in hospitals, orphanages, and schools. She appealed to women to exert themselves "with a patriotism at once firm and feminine for the greater good of all." And women listened.

Her didactic 1880 novel, *Coelebs in Search of a Wife*, which valorized a new kind of wise, effective, active, and responsible femininity, went into 11 editions in nine months and to 30 by the time of More's death. UCLA literary scholar Anne Mellor comments on the extent of More's influence:

> She urged her women readers to participate actively in the organization of voluntary benevolent societies and in the foundation of hospitals, orphanages, Sunday schools. . . . And her call was heard: literally thousands of voluntary societies sprang up in the opening decades of the nineteenth century to serve the needs of every imaginable group of sufferers.

It is hard to overstate the positive impact of widespread volunteerism on the fate of women. As women became engaged in charitable works, other parts of the public sphere became accessible. British historian F.K. Prochaska, in his seminal *Women and Philanthropy in Nineteenth-Century England* (1980), wrote, "The charitable experience of women was a lever which they used to open the doors closed to them in other spheres." According to Prochaska, as women began to become active in the outside world and form philanthropic organizations, they became interested in "government, administration and the law." Their volunteer work in charity schools focused their minds on education reform—for women of their own social class and for the poor women they sought to help. Prochaska, who calls More "probably the most influential woman of her day," concludes, "It should not come as a surprise that in 1866 women trained in charitable society were prominent among those who petitioned the House of Commons praying for the enfranchisement of their sex."

It was taken for granted in More's time that women were less intelligent and less serious than men, and thus unworthy of the Enlightenment rights and privileges of men. More flatly rejected these assumptions. But she did so without rejecting the idea of a special women's sphere. She embraced that sphere, giving it greater dignity and power. That was her signature Burkean style of feminism. More initiated a humane revolution in the relations of the sexes that was decorous, civilized, and in no way socially divisive. Above all, it was a feminism that women themselves could comfortably embrace, a feminism that granted women the liberty to be themselves without ceasing to be women. Indeed, if More's name and fame had not been brushed out of women's history, many women today might well be identifying with a modernized version of her female-friendly feminism.

Fortunately, her ideals and her style of feminism are well represented in the novels of Jane Austen. We don't know for sure whether Austen read More, but scholars claim to see the unmistakable influence in her writings of both More and Wollstonecraft. Her heroines are paragons of rational, merciful, and responsible womanhood. Austen also honors a style of enlightened and chivalrous manhood. Austen's heroes—men like Mr. Darcy, Captain Wentworth, and Mr. Knightly—esteem female strength, rationality, and intelligence.

Egalitarian feminists like Wollstonecraft (and later, John Stuart Mill and Harriet Taylor) are staple figures in the intellectual history of feminism, but they have never attracted a very large following among rank-and-file women of their time. More succeeded brilliantly with all classes of women. She awakened a nation and changed the way it saw itself. What she achieved was unprecedented. But the feminist scholar Elizabeth Kowalski-Wallace speaks for many when she describes More as being like the "uninvited guest" who "makes the process of celebrating our history as women more difficult."

The penchant of ideological scholars to denigrate or delete conservatives from the official "herstorical" record has not been confined to Hannah More. Ken Burns, the celebrated documentarian, followed his award-winning *Civil War* with a 1999 film about Elizabeth Cady Stanton (1815–1902) and Susan B. Anthony (1820–1906) and their struggle to win the vote for American women. There is one brief sequence in which the narrator explains that in the last quarter of the 19th century, Anthony forged coalitions with conservative mainstream groups. The mood of the film darkens, and a pioneer in the field of women's studies—Professor Sally Roesch Wagner— appears on the screen. Wagner informs viewers that Anthony was so determined to win the vote that she established alliances with pro-suffrage women who were "enemies of freedom in every other way—Frances Willard is a case in point." The camera then shows a photo of a menacing-looking Willard.

One would never imagine from Burns's film that Frances Willard (1839–1898) was one of the most beloved and respected women of the 19th century. When she died, one newspaper wrote, "No woman's name is better known in the English speaking world than that of Miss Willard, save that of England's great queen." Because of her prodigious good works and kindly nature, Willard was often called the "Saint Frances of American Womanhood."

But Willard, a suffragist and leader of the Christian Women's Temperance Union, is another once-esteemed figure in women's history who is today unmentioned and unmentionable. Willard brought mainstream women into the suffrage movement, and some historians credit her with doing far more to win the vote for women than any other suffragist. But her fondness for saying things like "Womanliness first—afterwards what you will" was her ticket to historical oblivion.

Acceptable feminist founders like Elizabeth Cady Stanton and Susan B. Anthony promoted women's suffrage through appeals to universal rights. They were inspired by John Locke, Mary Wollstonecraft, and Thomas Jefferson. Stanton wrote affectingly on "the individuality of each human soul" and on a woman's need to be the "arbiter of her own destiny." She and her sister suffragists brought a feminist Enlightenment to women, but, to their abiding disappointment, American women greeted the offer with a mixture of indifference and hostility. Stanton's words were effective with a relatively small coterie of educated women, mostly on the East Coast. When a suffrage amendment failed dismally in the state of Colorado in 1877, one newspaper editorial called the suffragists "carpetbaggers" promoting an elitist "eastern issue." The headline read: "Good-bye to the Female Tramps of Boston."

For many decades the average American woman simply ignored the cause of suffrage. In her *History of Women's Suffrage*, Anthony wrote that "in the indifference and inertia, the apathy of women, lies the greatest obstacle to their enfranchisement." Later, in the 1880s and 1890s, many women actively organized against it. Stanford historian Carl Degler, in his classic social history, *At Odds: Women and the Family in America From the Revolution to the Present* (1981), notes that in 1890 more than 20,000 women had joined an anti-suffrage group in New York State alone.

To prove once and for all that the majority of women wanted the vote, suffragists organized a referendum in Massachusetts in 1895. Both men and women were allowed to take part. The initiative lost: there were 187,000 votes opposed to granting women the franchise and only 110,000 in favor. Of those who voted yes, only 23,000 were women! In their history of the suffrage movement, Anthony and her co-author Ida Harper wrote, "The average man would not vote against granting women the suffrage if all those of his own family brought a strong pressure to bear upon him in its favor." It is the conventional wisdom that men denied women the ballot. But even a cursory look at the historical record suggests that men were not the problem.

Degler and other historians believe that because the vote was associated with individualism and personal assertiveness, many women saw it as both selfish and an attack on their unique and valued place in the family. The cult of domesticity had freed many rural women from manual labor, improved the material conditions of women's lives, and coincided with an increase in female life expectancy. Furthermore, as Degler shows, in 19th-century America both the public and private spheres were prized and valued. The companionate marriages described by Jane Austen were the American domestic ideal. Alexis de Tocqueville commented on the essential equality of the male and female spheres in his *Democracy in America* (1840): "Americans," he said, "did not think that men and women should perform the same tasks, but they show an equal regard for both their perspective parts; and though their lot is different, they consider both of them as being of equal value."

Hence as long as women saw the vote as a threat to their sphere, suffrage was a lost cause. Impassioned feminist rhetoric about freedom, dignity, autonomy, and individual rights fell on deaf ears. If the American women's movement was going to move forward, the suffrage movement needed new arguments and new ways of thinking that were more respectful and protective of women's role. Frances Willard showed the way.

Frances Willard served as president of the Women's Christian Temperance Union from 1879 until her death in 1898. Under her leadership it grew to be the largest and most influential women's organization in the nation. Today we associate temperance with Puritanism. But in the late 19th century, most feminists, including Elizabeth Cady Stanton and Susan B. Anthony, supported it. Temperance advocates believed that a ban on the sale of alcohol would greatly diminish wife abuse, desertion, destitution, and crime. In other words, temperance was a movement in defense of the home— the sphere of female freedom.

Willard was proud of women's role as the "angel in the house." But why, she asked, limit these angels to the home? With the vote, said Willard, women could greatly increase their civilizing and humane influence on society. With the vote, they could protect the homes they so dearly loved. Indeed, Willard referred to the "vote" as the "the home protection ballot." Women were moved by this, and men were disarmed.

Anthony admired Willard; Stanton, a skeptic in religious matters, was leery. Both were startled by her ability to attract unprecedented numbers of dedicated women to the suffrage cause. The membership figures for the various women's organizations are striking. In 1890, two leading egalitarian suffragist groups merged because they were worried that the cause was dying. They formed the National American Woman Suffrage Association and elected Elizabeth Cady Stanton president. The total membership of these combined groups, according to University of Michigan historian Ruth Bordin, was 13,000. By comparison, Willard had built an organization with more than ten times that number: by 1890 she had 150,000 adult dues-paying members. Moreover, Willard and her followers began to bring the suffrage movement something new and unprecedented—victories.

In 1893 the state of Colorado held a second election on women's suffrage. Unlike 1877, when the suffragists lost and the so-called "tramps of Boston" were sent packing, this time the suffragists won the vote by a 55 percent majority. Most historians agree that Willard's new conservative approach explains the success. She had persuaded large numbers of men and women that it was a mother's sacred duty to vote.

Thomas Carlyle has ascribed the insights of genius to "cooperation with the tendency of the world." Like Hannah More before her, Willard cooperated with the world and discerned novel and effective ways to improve it. Feminists do not honor the memory of these women. Indeed, with the exception of a small group of professional historians and literary critics, almost no one knows who they are. Still, it is interesting to note, today the Hannah More/Frances Willard style of conservative feminism is on the verge of a powerful resurgence.

In her 1990 book, *In Search of Islamic Feminism*, the University of Texas Middle Eastern studies professor Elizabeth Warnock Fernea has described a new style of feminism coming to life throughout the Muslim world. Traveling through Uzbekistan, Saudi Arabia, Morocco, Turkey, and Iraq, Fernea met great numbers of women's advocates working hard to improve the status of women. There have always been Western-style egalitarian feminists in these countries. But they are small in number and tend to be found among the most educated elites. The "Islamic feminists" Fernea was meeting were different. They were traditional, religious, and family-centered—and they had a following among women from all social classes. They were proud of women's role as mother, wife, and caregiver. Several rejected what they see as divisiveness in today's American women's movement. As one Iraqi women's advocate, Haifa Abdul Rahman, told her, "We see feminism in America as dividing women from men, separating women from the family. This is bad for everyone." Fernea settled on the term "family feminism" to describe this new movement. Experts on the history of Western feminism will here recognize its affinities with Frances Willard's long-lost teachings. Today, almost 20 years after Fernea's book, conservative feminism is surging in the Muslim world.

When Frances Willard died in 1898, her younger feminist colleague Carrie Chapman Catt remarked, "There has never been a woman leader in this country greater than Frances Willard." But today's feminists remain implacably hostile to Willard's notions of "womanly virtue" and have no sympathy with her family-centered feminism. These are unforgivable defects in their eyes, but they are precisely the traits that make Willard's style of feminism highly relevant to the many millions of women all over the world who are struggling for their rights and freedoms in strongly traditional societies, and who do not want to be liberated from their love for family, children, and husband.

Truth be told, there are also great numbers of contemporary American women who would today readily label themselves as feminists were they aware of a conservative alternative, in which liberty rather than "liberation" is the dominant idea. Today, more than

70 percent of American women reject the label "feminist," largely because the label has been appropriated by those who hate the very idea of a feminine sphere.

Clare Boothe Luce, a conservative feminist who in her heyday in the 1940s was a popular playwright and a member of the United States Congress, wrote and spoke about women at a time when feminism's Second Wave was still more than 20 years away. Luce's exemplary remarks on Mother Nature and sex differences are especially relevant today.

> It is time to leave the question of the role of women in society up to Mother Nature—a difficult lady to fool. You have only to give women the same opportunities as men, and you will soon find out what is or is not in their nature. What is in women's nature to do they will do, and you won't be able to stop them. But you will also find, and so will they, that what is not in their nature, even if they are given every opportunity, they will not do, and you won't be able to make them do it.

Camille Paglia once told me she found these words "absolutely awe-inspiring." So do I. Luce takes the best of both equal rights and conservative feminism. She is careful to say that women's nature can be made known only in conditions of freedom and opportunity. It is in such conditions of respect and fairness that woman can reveal their true preferences. Clearly Luce does not expect that women will turn out to be interchangeable with men.

When Luce wrote her cautionary words, sex role stereotypes still powerfully limited women's choices and opportunities. Today, women enjoy the equality of opportunity that Luce alluded to. The conventional constraints, confinements, and rigid expectations are largely things of the past. It is now possible to observe "the role of women in society" by taking note of the roles women themselves freely choose. Was Wollstonecraft right to insist that under conditions of freedom the sexes would make similar choices? Or was Hannah More closer to the truth when she suggested that women will always prevail in the private sphere and express themselves as the natural caregivers of the species?

We know from common observation that women are markedly more nurturing and empathetic than men. The female tendency to be empathic and caring shows up very early in life. Female infants, for example, show greater distress and concern than male infants over the plight of others; this difference persists into adulthood. Women don't merely say they want to help others; they enter the helping and caring professions in great numbers. Even today, in an era where equal rights feminism is dominant in education, the media, and the women's movement, women continue to be vastly over-represented in fields such as nursing, social work, pediatrics, veterinary medicine, and early childhood education. The great 19th-century psychologist William James said that for men "the world is a theater for heroism." That may be an overstatement, but it finds a lot of support in modern social science—and the evidence of everyday life. Women are numerically dominant in the helping professions; men prevail in the saving and rescuing vocational roles—policemen, firefighters, and soldiers.

Here we come to the central paradox of equal rights feminism: when women are liberated from the domestic sphere and no longer forced into the role of nurturers, when they are granted their full Lockean/Jeffersonian freedoms to pursue happiness in all the multitudinous ways a free society has to offer, many, perhaps most, if you count the adaptives, still give priority to the domestic sphere.

In a 1975 exchange in the *Saturday Review*, the feminist pioneer Betty Friedan and the French philosopher and women's rights advocate Simone de Beauvoir discussed the "problem" of stay-at-home mothers. Friedan told Beauvoir that she believed women should have the choice to stay home to raise their children if that is what they wish to do. Beauvoir candidly disagreed:

No, we don't believe that any woman should have this choice. No woman should be authorized to stay at home to raise her children. Society should be totally different. Women should not have that choice, precisely because if there is such a choice, too many women will make that one . . .

For Beauvoir, women who chose to be conventional wives and mothers were *eo ipso* benighted and in need of consciousness raising and re-socialization. Her intolerance and condescension toward family-centered women is shared by many in today's feminist establishment. And this intolerance has affected the education of American students. In all the women's studies texts studied in a recent survey by Christine Rosen, without exception traditional marriage, stay-at-home mothers, and the culture of romance come under heavy fire. Domesticity is slighted if not ridiculed or savaged. In other words, the sphere of life that has the greatest appeal to most women, and is inseparable from traditional ideas of feminine fulfillment, is rejected, if not outright forbidden, by the self-appointed liberators. In Simone de Beauvoir we see how starkly the ideology of liberation is opposed to the pursuit of liberty.

Today, the feminist establishment in the United States is dominated by the radical wing of the egalitarian tradition. Not only do its members not cooperate with their conservative sisters—they often denigrate and vilify them; indeed, they have all but eliminated them from the history of American feminism. Revisionist history is never a pretty sight. But feminist revisionists are destructive in special ways. It is not only history that they wish to obliterate, but also women themselves.

My friendly advice to serious establishment feminists is to make peace with Hannah More and Frances Willard and their modern-day heirs—or face a complete loss of popularity and effectiveness. Eve Ensler and her most devoted disciple, Jane Fonda, may not be amenable to change. But there is hope for the younger generation. Over the years, I have lectured on more than a hundred college campuses where I meet both conservative and radical young women activists. It is the former who invite me; the latter come to jeer and wrangle. But as a rule, we all part as friends. "Why do you like *The Vagina Monologues* so much?" I ask them. Most of them tell me that by acting in the play or supporting it, they are both having fun and serving a good cause. (Funds raised by the performances go to support local domestic violence shelters.) Few young women seem to be buying the underlying "philosophy."

These young women can be reasoned with, and many of them seem to be fully capable of forming a coalition with moderate and conservative women to work for their common interest. My advice to them: Don't bother "taking back the Garden." Take back feminism. Restore its lost history. Make the movement attractive once again to the silent majority of American women, who really don't want to be liberated from their womanhood. And then take on the cause of the women who have yet to find the liberty that all women everywhere deserve.

Liberty and the Nation State

Jeremy Rabkin

International courts, trans-national institutions, multinational corporations, universal religions, all ride roughshod over the sovereign claims of the nation state. But none of them is able to provide what the nation state provides, which is territorial sovereignty and the freedoms guaranteed by secure borders and a rule of law within them. Jeremy Rabkin, professor of law at George Mason University, shows that it is to the nation state that we owe our fundamental liberties, and that threats to its sovereignty are also threats to the freedom of the individual.

In the past, freedom was often conceived as an attribute of persons. The free man could exercise free thought and free will. He was the opposite of the slave—of the man enslaved by others, or the man enslaved by his passions, his superstitions, his bodily needs. Today we more often think of freedom as an attribute of places. We refer to a "free country" or a "free society" or (as the Second Amendment to our Constitution puts it) a "free state." To view it this way implies that freedom is not so much a challenge one must live up to as a place to which one can move. In fact, tens of millions of people have moved from tyrannical states and empires over the past three centuries in search of better lives. And almost always they moved to free nations. If freedom has a natural home in the modern world, therefore, it is the nation state, the legal entity that claims sovereignty within a bounded territory and that can grant freedom within that territory through its law. It is very hard to imagine the survival of freedom in a world that has left the nation state behind.

WORLD GOVERNMENT?

You can see the point most easily if you think about the most commonly discussed alternatives to nation states. Start with world government. Today the phrase sounds somewhat quaint, a sort of Edwardian fantasy from the fountain pen of a faded seer like H. G. Wells. But Wells was still writing on this theme on the eve of the conference that drafted the U.N. Charter in 1945. As late as the early 1950s, the World Federalist Society—dedicated to promoting some version of Wells's science fiction vision—included in its ranks prominent members of the U.S. Congress. In the mid-1960s, the World Federalists were even able to persuade Chief Justice Earl Warren to address their convention (where he spoke in praise of the U.N.).

The most obvious objection to world government was stated in medieval times. The Florentine poet and thinker Dante Alighieri offered a utopian vision for earthly government, lauding, in his tract *De Monarchia,* the peace and prosperity that would follow when the entire world submitted to the rule of one empire. The work was denounced by the Church: Dante assumed, his clerical critics argued, that divine attributes (such as omniscience and absolute benevolence) could be found in mere earthly rulers.

The objection remains valid. What makes for freedom is not the extent of government or its lack of national boundaries but the way in which government is exercised. If there were a world government, why wouldn't it simply end up as a world tyranny? In modern times, the most respected philosopher to embrace something like world government was Immanuel Kant. And Kant insisted, in his plan for a world peace federation, that the federation must limit its

114

role to maintaining peace among nations, each of which should be an autonomous republic, under its own internal rule of law. (That is why Kant called the federation he proposed a "League of Nations.") Other plans for world government, such as those of the socialist and communist "internationals," have brushed all such considerations aside.

But Kant's vision too is defective. For if a world authority has enough power to guarantee every nation against its enemies, it must be more powerful than any of its component nations. So what power could compel it to limit its reach? Suppose a particular state thought the federation was exceeding its rightful role. Could that state withdraw from the peace federation? If so, wouldn't that undermine the hope for uniting all states in one global peace federation? If not, wouldn't that leave the federation to keep expanding its powers, despite any objections from individual member states? Or would a universal peace federation simply transfer the old threat of war between states into a new threat of civil war within the universal federation?

Good questions, even today. The U.N. Charter, as formulated in 1945, envisioned a limited, modified version of the peace federation. The Security Council was to have military forces on call, including an international bomber command for quick action. As these provisions were adopted only a few weeks after the firebombing of Dresden, one may assume the delegates had some fairly severe "action" in mind, at least as an ultimate threat. Nothing of the sort ever developed, of course. Even when the end of the Cold War brought talk of a "new world order," there were not many voices urging that the new order be entrusted with an international bomber force, for the very reason that any international force would reflect the priorities of its most determined members. The U.N. has never endorsed military confrontations to end tyranny or even mass slaughter. The U.N. sat passively on the sidelines while 800,000 Tutzis were slaughtered in Rwanda in 1994. When NATO launched its bombing campaign against Serbia in 1999, to end murder and repression in Kosovo, it acted without U.N. sanction because Russia and China vetoed proposals for U.N. authorization. Even in Afghanistan, where the U.N. did authorize military action in 2001, the forces that actually overthrew the Taliban regime (and have continued to fight on behalf of the new democratic government) were supplied by the United States and a small number of our NATO allies. Such examples show that an international force can uphold the concerns of free nations only if controlled by free nations.

In short, either a world authority has dominant force on its side or we remain in a world where lesser powers have the last word. Today, almost all those powers are territorial states. The European Union, which claims to transcend national differences, has turned out to be of little relevance on great issues of war and peace. All its members have endorsed the war in Afghanistan, but some EU nations (notably Britain, Poland, and the Netherlands) have cooperated with U.S. military efforts there, while others (notably France and Germany) have refused to allow their troops to take part in the fighting.

France and Germany tried to mobilize opposition to the U.S.-led invasion of Iraq in 2003, but Britain and a majority of other EU states joined the U.S. coalition. In some EU states that originally supported the war, elections brought new governments that decided to withdraw their troops from the coalition (as with Spain and Italy). In other countries (such as Britain, the Netherlands, and Denmark), elections confirmed public support for governments that continued their military commitments in Iraq. The EU, as such, has contributed little more than background noise. When it comes to vital questions of war and peace, states can make hard decisions, while trans-national entities merely engage in discussions.

Of course, not all territorial states are democracies. Multinational empires have found it particularly hard to maintain democratic governments. In the late 19th century, when most states in western Europe had developed parliamentary forms of government, the Austrian Empire tried to join the trend. Representatives from different ethnic communities not only could not manage to form stable majorities but also could not manage to keep their disputes from descending into actual violence in the parliament building. So the empire was ruled by bureaucratic decree until it finally collapsed into separate national states. The old Soviet Union managed to keep "captive nations" under its rule by ruthless repression until it too collapsed into separate national states in 1990. Fear of separatist movements—combining with others to overthrow the government or trying to leave the country and taking their part of its territory with them—remains a motive for repression in a number of countries today, most notably China. Even democratic countries have sometimes found it hard to conciliate ethnic differences, leading to the actual breakup of Czechoslovakia and Yugoslavia in the 1990s and persistent demands for independence or at least greater autonomy in Quebec.

How much simpler if all people could be satisfied by the same international standards! And if the United Nations could solve the problem of conflict between nations, why not also remove the grounds for conflict within each nation by assuring all people everywhere of the same human rights? The U.N. Charter accordingly included vague references to "promoting human rights" among the U.N.'s fundamental goals. Over the past 60 years, the organization has indeed promoted dozens of human rights standards.

Some are quite proper (such as provisions for "freedom of worship"); some are vapid (such as provisions guaranteeing the right to vote, without mentioning the right of rival parties to field competing candidates); some are silly (such as requirements to ensure that jobs held by women are compensated in accord with their "worth").

The world's worst tyrannies have readily ratified these conventions—and eagerly taken their part in "monitoring" compliance and deflecting scrutiny from themselves. In a forum that gives the same participation rights to tyrannies and free nations, "human rights" protection has never maintained a steady focus on the worst tyrannies. So the U.N. has contributed almost nothing to the advancement of freedom in the world. Even in Europe, where a regional Convention on Human Rights was established by Western nations and counts a solid majority of Western-style democracies in its membership, Russia has been a member in good standing since the 1990s—and seems to have been restrained not at all in its subsequent slide toward authoritarian rule.

In short, just as we still rely on nation states for international security, we must still rely on national governments to protect individual rights. Your freedom still depends on where you live.

THE STRENGTH OF NATIONS

The nation state, as we think of it today, is a product of modern times, emerging from the breakup of empires and from declarations of independence made by people wishing to claim their familiar territory as a home. In fact, the world's most successful nation state—certainly its richest and freest—was founded on just such a declaration. The American Declaration of Independence asserted that when subject to intolerable abuses, "one people may dissolve the political bands which have [previously] connected them with another." The Declaration refers to the people of Britain as "brethren," presumably in view of common origins. But it goes on, in its penultimate paragraph, to insist that the American states will henceforth hold the British "as we hold the rest of mankind, enemies in war, in peace friends." That is what independence means: national governments speak for the actual citizens of their own countries, not for groups defined without reference to national boundaries.

The Declaration of Independence is clear that nations are grounded in the consent of their current members rather than in mere ancestry. The Declaration even cites as one of the "causes" that "impelled [Americans] to the separation" from Britain that the British government had "endeavored to prevent the population of these states" by "obstructing laws for the naturalization of foreigners, refusing to pass others to encourage their migration hither

. . ." So the Declaration envisions the United States as a place of refuge, to which people may come to enjoy the benefits of freedom under law.

Little more than a decade later, *The Federalist* urged the necessity of a "national government." The very first article acknowledged that—despite the principles asserted in the Declaration of Independence—governments founded in consent were so rare in the world that "it seems to have been reserved to the people of this country, by their conduct and example, to decide the important question, whether societies of men are really capable or not of establishing good government from reflection and choice, or whether they are forever destined to depend for their political constitution on accident and force."

In the history of the world, most people, most of the time, had lived in accord with the customs and folkways of their clan, tribe, village, or religion—with lives largely determined by the circumstances into which they happened to be born. Often they were incorporated into larger kingdoms or great empires, although even these larger structures usually ruled through local chiefs, elders, or warlords, with highest honors allocated to the most successful conquerors. When the United States was founded, it was not even generally accepted in Europe that distinct nations should have their own governments. Much of the continent still lived under the rule of multinational empires—most notably the Romanovs and Ottomans in the East, the Hapsburgs in central Europe.

All the more striking, then, that *The Federalist* argued not just for government by consent but for government on a national basis. The second paper in the series (by John Jay, subsequently first Chief Justice of the Supreme Court) suggests a kind of divinely appointed destiny for the new nation: "Providence has been pleased to give this one connected country to one united people—a people descended from the same ancestors, speaking the same language, professing the same religion, attached to the same principles of government, very similar in their manners and customs . . ."

The authors did not lay too much stress on divine providence, however. The Constitution advocated by *The Federalist* includes a prohibition on religious tests for office, along with authorization for Congress to "establish a uniform rule of naturalization" (that is, legislation to make foreigners into American citizens) that indicates no limits on eligibility.

While the Constitution requires the president to be "a natural born citizen," it allows naturalized citizens to serve in the House of Representatives, the Senate, and the Supreme Court—as happened, in fact, from the earliest days of the Constitution. Nearly half of the ensuing papers in *The Federalist* belabor the argument that, without a strong common government—a national government— the American confederacy will break into regional confederacies, which might not only descend to war with one another but also seek foreign assistance and so become perpetually entangled in foreign wars. The final paper in the series concludes that "a nation without a national government is an awful spectacle." The underlying argument, in short, is that a nation is not simply a given, not an inescapable destiny, but a human creation—something maintained by "reflection and choice."

We should give due weight to the term "reflection" here. Apart from tribes and empires, the Western world still remembered the experience of the self-governing states of ancient Greece and Rome. Almost all Western languages (and many non-Western languages) have adopted the term "politics" from the Greek *polis* and "republic" from the Roman *res publica*—words preserved from dead languages because they did not have living models. What sustained such embedded reminders of the ancient republics was the appeal of citizens taking an active part in openly debating and then openly deciding how their community should be governed. Modern nations had reason to look back on the ancient republics with mixed feelings, however.

In the ancient republics, sizable parts of the population were held in slavery, or helotry, or excluded from citizenship as "foreigners" *(metoikoi),* even if born into the territory of a particular city state. Those who were citizens took part in "politics"—but often very extreme politics, as leaders of contending factions imposed execution or exile on rivals and bolder usurpations provoked bloodier civil strife. *The Federalist* stressed the point: "It is impossible to read the history of the petty republics of Greece and Italy without feeling sensations of horror and disgust at the distractions with which they were continually agitated and . . . [their] perpetual vibration between the extremes of tyranny and anarchy."

There was, one could say, too much choice—for both political communities and their leading citizens. *The Federalist* several times remarks on the readiness of leaders of republics to betray their countries out of personal ambition—evidently alluding to the "noble lives" recounted by Plutarch. They looked for a more stable sense of nationality to support a more stable form of politics.

Government by consent doesn't mean government with which all citizens agree. It means government with which citizens may freely disagree. This is the great achievement of Western constitutional democracy. If the constitutional safeguards that secure my basic freedoms are in place, then I can proceed with my life regardless of those in high office; I can freely disagree with them, as they cannot punish me for doing so. Much of *The Federalist* celebrates the division of powers between the federal government and the states. Still more papers defend the separation of powers and the constitutional guarantees of individual rights. But in the end, the force of the Constitution relies on the claim that "we the people"—collectively—stand behind it. And that theoretical claim is much easier to embrace if there is some degree of national unity in the background. Even in the 19th century, the United States was sympathetic to independence movements of other peoples. While presidents tried to keep official foreign policy free of entanglement in foreign disputes, members of Congress were quick to express sympathy for the Greeks in their war to throw off Turkish domination, for Polish rebellions against Russia, for Hungarian and then Italian rebellions against Austrian control.

Woodrow Wilson's support for "national self-determination"—that is, the breakup of the multinational empires—at the end of World War I was almost foreordained. Senate critics of the Versailles Treaty wasted no tears on the vanished empires; rather, they complained that it was wrong to have imposed artificial boundaries on some of the new states—and wrong to have acceded to continuing foreign enclaves in China. They believed that enduring democracies could arise only where there were also nation states to support them.

POLITICAL COSTS OF SUPRANATIONALISM

The emergence of the nation state facilitated the spread of democracy by identifying bounded territories with the people who lived in them. In contemporary Europe, however, nationalism provokes shudders, being blamed for "centuries of conflict" culminating in two world wars, while the European Union is credited by its defenders with delivering peace. In 2005, during debate over the proposed new constitutional treaty for the EU, commissioner Margot Wallstrom, vice-president of the European Commission, went so far as to warn that if the constitutional treaty were defeated, Europe would be at risk for new genocide. Just who would be killing whom she did not say. But, in the spirit of harmony and continental understanding, she embraced the European convention according to which the unique crimes of the Germans resulted exclusively from "nationalism"—as if Belgium or Portugal were always on the verge of invading their neighbors or Sweden (Wallstrom's home country) in danger of exterminating the ethnic Finns.

But if the European Union is hostile to nationalism, it is not really hostile to the nation state. Indeed, it depends on the nation states for its survival. It is not simply that it has no army. It has no police. It has no criminal law or criminal courts of its own. It does not even have field agents. All its policies must be implemented by national governments, so that citizens feel the sting of EU policies only through the pinch of enforcement actions by national officials in their own countries.

Major EU policies must be approved by a council of ministers from member governments. In many areas, policies can be established even when not all governments approve, but there must be a "qualified majority"—in a system that gives extra votes to more populous states but requires majorities of both governments and population-weighted votes. The European Commission proposes new policies for the council of ministers and then prepares detailed implementing regulations for national governments. The European Court of Justice hears appeals from national courts to clarify the meaning of EU treaties and standards, leaving national courts to work out applications in particular cases.

But the EU does not have a genuine government of its own. There is a directly elected parliament, but its powers are limited to rejecting major measures. Although successive treaties have tinkered with details, there has never been a serious proposal to give the same powers to the European Parliament that parliaments have in all the member states. To do so would be to admit that all smaller states could be outvoted and overwhelmed by the European majority, like rural counties in a national parliament.

So the EU, while acquiring a very broad range of powers, is not trusted to exercise some of the most fundamental powers of government. It is mostly financed from European-wide tariffs and lacks separate taxing authority. Compared to national governments, it has very little revenue and (apart from agricultural subsidies and some development subsidies to less affluent members) very little spending responsibility. It is not trusted to administer retirement pensions, health insurance, school finance, or other major responsibilities of national governments. It has no separate executive to provide leadership in a crisis, but merely a "president"—the prime minister of a member state serving for six months until all members (including Luxembourg) have had their chance rotating through the half-year "presidency." The proposed new constitution for Europe sought to strengthen the office by giving it a three-year term and election by other prime ministers instead of automatic rotation, but it did not propose any serious increase in powers to the office.

So the EU does not supplant the member states but feeds off their legitimacy. The parliament has never developed parties of its own. Candidates compete as members of national parties that then form loose alliances within the European parliament. The most visible and engaging aspects of public life—the sorts of things that get most attention in national media—are lacking in the EU. There is no great wrangling among contending parties and contending interests on big questions of allocation—the prizes in legislative and electoral politics. There are no dramatic initiatives to handle a crisis or mobilize support for a bold new project—the stuff of executive leadership. Almost everything gets swallowed in technical details of bureaucratic directives or judicial interpretations.

And here, surely, lies the growing crisis within the European institutions. Established as an alternative to the nation state, the EU depends on the nation states for its precarious legitimacy. At the same time, its powers—exerted by an unelected European Commission and a parliament that can do little except veto the Commission's measures—are resented by national electorates, so much so that, in the rerun of the treaty for a constitution, the European leaders have done their utmost to prevent referendums in the member states. The Irish, obliged by their own constitution to have such a referendum, decisively rejected the treaty in June of 2008, though of course the Irish people were told that their vote could not be accepted, and that they must vote again.

Moreover, officials in national governments estimate that more than half of the legal standards they enforce today are actually derived from EU mandates. A body that imposes such an enormous legislative burden on people who have no say in controlling it will not inspire loyalty. Indeed, citizens of the nation states regard the EU as so far from making any real claim on their allegiance that most do not bother to vote in elections to its parliament. In the EU we see a gradual confiscation of the powers of national governments without any corresponding accountability for their exercise. And the resulting deficit in legitimacy can be reversed only by acknowledging once again that legitimacy begins and ends in the nation state.

THE STAKES FOR LIBERTY

Meanwhile, in the United States, human rights advocates have been protesting American war policies for defying international humanitarian treaties, as these are read by the International Red Cross and Amnesty International. And the U.S. Supreme Court has, in a number of cases since 2002, invoked international treaties (including some not ratified by the U.S. Senate) and human rights rulings in foreign countries to determine what the U.S. Constitution should be interpreted to require.

It may seem ironic that trans-national impulses have gathered momentum in the United States just as they have been faltering in Europe. But in a way it is logical. The great historic achievement of the nation state has been to create political space for open debate. Citizens may disagree in their outlook or ideological dispositions, but political debate in a nation state will be pulled back to common questions of safety and prosperity. If you want to escape political debate, it makes sense (in a way) to embrace some imagined consensus of mankind, which can appear more consensual and unified the more abstract it is. So almost no one urges that the U.N. be stripped of responsibility for protecting human rights, even though the U.N. Human Rights Council, now chaired by Cuba, has decided to concentrate on the threat of Islamophobia in Western countries rather than mass murder in Sudan. But the abstract idea of world concern for human rights is so edifying—and amorphous—that it shields the U.N. from any serious assessment of its performance. The EU floats in a similar cloud of protective abstractions, being less like a government than a church—an entity supposed to inspire proper attitudes rather than take responsibility for actual results.

Perhaps none of this would matter if free countries in the world faced an untroubled future in which most decisions could be safely delegated to technical specialists. But that is not the situation. Lower birth rates and rising life spans mean government pension and health care systems will face increasingly sharp strains. This problem is particularly serious in Europe, and although immigration might ease the problem, most European nations have had great difficulty integrating immigrants, particularly Muslim immigrants who have clustered in self-segregated communities. Within these communities, Islamists challenge the jurisdiction of European nation states and insist that within a few decades Europe will be governed by sharia. The European Union cannot secure the loyalty of immigrant communities, much less maintain necessary measures to detect and disrupt terror networks. Only nation states can hope to maintain the authority of law—and the personal freedoms, religious toleration, and open debate that are guaranteed by national legal systems. So the future of freedom in Europe will depend on the durability of its nation states.

Freedom and the City

Brian C. Anderson

The idea of the free citizen has its root in the Greek city state, and throughout Western history it has been in the cities that liberties have been defined, upheld, and expanded. Brian C. Anderson, editor of New York's City Journal, *devoted to upholding urban life and its lasting values, here shows the way in which liberty has been woven into the fabric of the Western city.*

"Civilization as we know it is inseparable from urban life," wrote Friedrich Hayek in his classic study *The Constitution of Liberty,* and by civilization he meant the Western kind. The Austrian economist viewed the city as the source of the West's dynamic, world-transforming science, culture, and prosperity. The "bourgeois" values of civility and urbanity are also products of the city, and ultimately (although Hayek did not develop this theme) it is to the city that we owe the liberty that has been embodied in our political, spiritual, and economic institutions. Simply put, without the city, no democracy, no Christianity, no capitalism, no West.

The city's importance in Western civilization makes its long crisis deeply troubling. In the second half of the 20th century, blight, crime, and ugliness have ravaged many American and European urban areas, and have reached them all. The crisis represents, I believe, a general loss of Western self-confidence; I will explore a few of its causes and point to some welcome signs of renewal.

The word "politics" derives from *polis*, the Greek word for the city state, of which Athens was the leading example. The "Greek miracle," as Philippe Nemo describes it in his important recent book *What Is the West?*, was in essence political—the great philosophical and artistic achievements of the Athenians being a byproduct of their political freedom. The Greek city arose in the eighth century B.C. out of the ruins of the Mycenaean civilization, which had been based on divine kingship. Urban republics took the place of monarchy; participatory rule replaced the shadowy machinations of the royal palace. "The powers of ruling officials in the Greek City became an open, public matter," writes Nemo—as is shown by the archaeological evidence of the Athenian agora, the public square where citizens would gather to deliberate their communal ends.

Religion, too, surrendered to the democratic city some of its social and moral authority, which in archaic times had been absolute, unchanging, demanding complete submission. Why the agora happened when and where it did is anybody's guess, since history records no earlier example. It does seem a kind of miracle, an irruption or mutation in the order of time. But happen it did. In the agora, noble lineage or sacred position mattered less than a man's debating skills, especially his ability to make persuasive arguments. Because any citizen, even the lowliest, could make such arguments, a new conception of the human person emerged—a conception that has been internalized by Western civilization. As Nemo puts it, we have inherited from Greek democracy the idea of "each one as the equal of all others, before the law, subject to law, and helping to write the law." The aristocratic virtues associated with the era of Homeric kingship were increasingly seen as excessive and violent. Moderation and reason emerged as core values of the polis.

On a deeper level, the Greeks discovered the distinction between nature and convention—between *phusis* and *nomos*. Nature transcends the human will and constitutes the deep unalterable order of things; convention, however, is man-made and therefore open to change and reform. There is a natural law, implanted in the heart of things, but the laws that govern social life are conventional; they can be debated and, if found wanting, changed. And this is the premise of politics as we in the West have known it—not submission to a law that is unquestioned and eternal, but the creation of a law of our own, by rational deliberation and consent. In this way the "civic pillars" of modern constitutional states—the rule of man-made law, democracy and self-government, the rights and responsibilities of citizenship—were first erected. They would fall in the late Roman era, only to be rediscovered by Italian city states and then by modern English philosophers and statesmen. When we speak of "Athens" as central to the idea of the West, it is this philosophical architecture we have in mind. (One should not neglect in this context, however, the importance of theatrical spectacle to the Greek mind and to the Western experience. The theater creates the sense of an individual, living out the consequences of his free choices, though trapped, too, in fates beyond his control. The absence of an Islamic theater may have something to do with the Islamists' grim humorlessness, which reflects an inability to see themselves from outside, as we see actors in a drama.) The Greek philosophers held life in the city to be the only one that accorded with man's nature as a "political animal," as Aristotle famously defined him. In fact, Aristotle believed the city to be as natural as the family, and prior to it in importance. It is where a "rule of life" would make citizens "good and just" and help human beings to flourish. It is also of the right size—big enough that people could act collectively and have an effect on others, but not so big that citizens could not identify with one another, or love one another as friends.

Does such an understanding retain any meaning for modern constitutional democracies? The polis was a direct democracy, whose intrusions into private lives we would find unacceptably authoritarian; today, the will of the people leads to government action primarily by way of elected representatives. Moreover, contemporary thought, whether rightly or not, no longer accepts the Greek view that certain human ends are naturally superior to others. Human interests have become ever more varied, so that the notion of a common good is ever harder to conceive. Finally, our cities are not city states in the old sense.

They have long been subsumed by those larger sovereign bodies, nations, and many have become megacities, dwarfing in size even the largest urban centers of antiquity. The population of Athens at the height of its power, in the fifth and fourth centuries B.C., was probably around 300,000, with perhaps 70,000 adult males contending in the agora—fewer than populate Staten Island, New York City's smallest borough.

Nevertheless, our cities remain in some sense moral and political communities. In his classic 1981 study, *The Philosopher in the City*, constitutional scholar Hadley Arkes reminded us that the policy concerns of cities unavoidably go far beyond street cleaning and traffic regulation to encompass "questions of moral judgment which are far more important for . . . citizens in establishing the kind of people they wish to be." Cities answer such questions—on how to police and secure decent neighborhoods, how to educate children, how to encourage or discourage certain kinds of business, whether to tolerate "victimless" crimes like prostitution, and so on—in various ways. In America it is still often local government, not the nation as a whole, that answers those questions. Hence without republican virtues urban life as we know it will wither.

The other primal source of Western civilization also takes the shape of a city: Jerusalem, although maybe it would be more accurate to speak of Jerusalem as filtered through Rome. In his 2002 book *On Two Wings*, theologian Michael Novak argues that the political freedom of the Greek city would have had far less meaning without the triumph of "Jewish metaphysics." One major dimension of that metaphysics, he explains, is the biblical "narrative of purpose and progress." The pagan Greeks and Romans saw time as an inexorable cycle, repeating the same story again and again across millennia. By contrast, the Jews, and later the Christians, gave time a direction—a target. Time was seen as the dimension within which human liberty unfolds. It moves—though not inevitably, as reversals are certain—toward a new sacred kingdom, where love and justice will reign. Freedom matters in Jewish metaphysics, for it is what history is ultimately about: not political freedom only, as the Greeks had valued it, but inner freedom—the freedom of the will, which is (as the story of Genesis emphasizes) the foundation of the relationship between man and God.

"Liberty is the human condition established by the Bible, nearly every chapter of which turns upon the exercise of that freedom, as a wheel upon its axis," Novak writes. "What will Adam, King David, Peter, Saul do next? Liberty is the axis of the universe, the ground of the possibility of love, human and divine." Christianity would radicalize this emphasis on personal freedom, removing it from its communal context and extending it to all humanity. As a result, from the Confessions of St. Augustine to the novels of George Eliot and Henry James, personal liberty forms the leitmotif of Western literature. It is enshrined in our law, and especially in the common law of the English-speaking peoples, of which we in America are the great beneficiaries. It makes accountability and responsibility fundamental to all social and political relations. It has produced forms of education that encourage creativity and self-development rather than the submissive acceptance of routines.

These days we tend to look at history in the light of progress, the implicit goal of which is liberty. This attitude comes to us not from the Greeks or the Romans, or even from the Enlightenment, but, as Novak reminds us, "via the preaching of Jesus Christ, from whom the Gentiles learned the essential outlook of the Hebrews: that the Creator gave humans a special place among all other creatures, and made them free, and endowed them with incomparable responsibility and dignity." This metaphysical contribution of the Jews and Christians would never have shaped the history of Western civilization, however, if Christianity had not become a successful urban movement in the Roman Empire. All effective missionary movements are or swiftly become urban, because missionaries need to go where there are many potential converts. Hence St. Paul's journeys took in major cities, such as Antioch, Corinth, and Athens, and only occasionally smaller communities, like Iconium and Laodicea. No record exists of Paul preaching the Gospel in the countryside, even though all but 5 percent of the Roman Empire's population then lived in rural areas. The city collects agglomerations of people big enough to make conversion worthwhile. Several Greco-Roman urban centers in the era of early Christianity had populations in excess of 100,000, with two, Rome and Alexandria, climbing past 200,000. This concentration of people allowed reformers like Paul to reach a critical mass of potential converts, producing a viable subculture at odds with the prevailing norms of religious expression.

The evidence shows that by the time of Constantine's conversion in 312, Christians, having expanded to nine million in number, still made up only around 15 percent of the imperial population. However, almost all of them were urbanites, which greatly increased their political and communicative power. It was because their influence so far outstripped their numbers that Constantine sought the backing of the early church. The rest is history. But again: without cities, no Christendom—no West. Economic historians, such as Robert Lopez and, more recently, Avner Greif, have situated the birth of capitalism not, as the anti-Catholic Max Weber did, in the Protestant north of Europe and the Hanseatic League, but in the city states of Florence, Genoa, Venice, and other northern Italian urban centers during the Middle Ages. Emerging from an entropic Europe ravaged by barbarian invasions and Muslim ferocity, where Christian monks had kept the embers of classical civilization glowing, these urban republics—the first to exist since the polis—forged an economic empire that stretched as far as England, southern Russia, the oases of the Sahara Desert, India, and China. The world had never seen its like: a commercial revolution that was, according to Lopez, "probably the greatest turning point in the history of our civilization." This commercial revolution dissolved the old feudal system, freed serfs, and elevated a new elite, based on wealth rather than lineage or family: the bourgeoisie. A new literature and art was born; science and law, educational and cultural institutions all grew as prosperity spread. The modern ideals of liberty and equality began their long historical movement through Western institutions. The capitalist West had arrived, six centuries before the British Industrial Revolution gave modernity its current form. Lopez points to the separation of management from ownership of firms, the ceaseless effort to make firms more competitive, the expansion of credit, the accumulation of capital, the quest for profit, and various other aspects of full-blown capitalism.

As yet the transition all took place on a much smaller scale than would occur after the Industrial Revolution or during the rise of the global economy in the 20th century. And, as the word "bourgeois" conveys, it was an entirely urban phenomenon. But it was a decisive episode in the development of Western liberty.

What explains this commercial revolution?

First, free cities are often hothouses of economic growth. Urbanist Jane Jacobs has contended, plausibly to my mind, that virtually all economic development since the dawn of time has been generated in cities. By packing together so many people, often from different backgrounds and boasting a great variety of skills, urban agglomerations offer radical economic efficiencies—in a big city like New York, you can quickly get your hands on almost anything. Dense populations also fire creativity and invention, the true engines of wealth. Think of the fusion foods, the cultural inventions, the technological marvels, and the cornucopia of new goods that dynamic cities regularly produce. These urban advantages of efficiency and creativity are key reasons people continue to flood into cities,

133

despite the higher costs, both financial and stress-related, of urban life. More than half of the world's population is now urban, and this for a very good reason.

But there are other significant factors besides scale and variety. The Italian city states transformed themselves into the West's first economic dynamos largely because of the invention of effective, neutral institutions: banks, contracts, joint-stock companies, letters of credit, courts of appeal, and so on. These inventions established the framework for modern capitalism, by permitting trust between strangers, cooperation outside the family, and the ability of investors to secure assets.

That development raises a second question, however: why did these institutions arise first in the West? Greif, a professor at Stanford and a rising star of contemporary economic thought, argues that Western culture—the Western emphasis on the individual, born of Christianity—encouraged such innovations. Comparing the Christian Genoese with the Maghrebis, Jewish traders from North Africa who competed fiercely with the Italian city states for economic control of the 12th-century Mediterranean, Greif shows how the Maghrebis' thicker tribal relations held them back economically. They could raise money only from within the community, not in a credit market, like the Genoese, and their trading networks were familial as well, which limited their size compared with their Christian competitors, whose beliefs allowed them to extend far wider networks of trust. Maghrebi conflicts were not adjudicated in neutral courts like those of Genoa, and often culminated in violence and permanent banishments. Over time, the Maghrebis' communitarian approach to economic life proved less efficient and more fragile than the Genoese fidelity to rational institutions and the rule of law. In Greif's view, the West's institutional history is a long story of creating substitutes for the ties of the tribal family in just this way. This process is unthinkable without Christianity's trust-creating and culture-forming influence.

A few years ago, social scientist Rodney Stark concluded his book *The Victory of Reason* by quoting a Chinese scholar the Communist Party had tasked with leading a study group to understand the West's preeminence. "We studied everything we could from the historical, political, economic, and cultural perspective," the researcher said. "At first, we thought it was because you [the West] had more powerful guns than we had. Then we thought it was because you had the best political system. Next we focused on your economic system. But in the past 20 years, we have realized that the heart of your culture is your religion: Christianity. That is why the West is so powerful. The Christian moral foundation of social and cultural life was what made possible the emergence of capitalism and then the successful transition to democratic politics. We don't have any doubts about this."

A closely related component of the West's civilizational genius was brought to life in the trading cities of northern Italy: urbanity. "City air brings freedom," went an old saying dating from feudal times. In the nascent bourgeois cities, the personal bondage of feudalism dissolved, replaced by a new kind of solidarity among the traders and artisans, and soon among the lawyers, bankers, and others providing services to the proto-capitalist economy.

This solidarity based itself not on familial or religious obligation or on land ownership or birth in a caste or race but, instead, on rational economic interests and a demand for autonomy that soon translated itself into political terms. This solidarity was the matrix of modern civil society and the foundation of our democratic way of life.

This urban economic and civic culture offered citizens the chance to pursue material interests, to realize new rights and liberties, and to develop richer, more diverse personalities. We find this culture, at least a degree of it, wherever or whenever a Western city has since flourished. It arose only in the West, and Christianity's universalizing power is again the explanation. (Dutch social theorist

Anton Zijderveld traces this story artfully in his 1998 book, *A Theory of Urbanity*.) That the culture of urbanity might also work to loosen city dwellers from the duties of Christian faith—from faith in general—and thereby undermine its own foundations has been an irony of Western history. To talk about the culture of urbanity is to talk of the bourgeois virtues. These virtues—prudence, enterprise, fairness, hard work, sociability, honesty, thrift, self-possession, civility—are not those of the saint or the warrior. They stand to the warrior virtues as humility stands to pride. But by influencing and shaping the movements of a free economy, they have brought unprecedented prosperity, cooperation among strangers, social peace, and scientific and cultural progress. In a fallen world, they are more than defensible; from the standpoint of social order, they are the best we have yet devised, which is not to say that the virtues of the saint and the warrior are obsolete, for these too are needed if a society is to confront natural disasters and external threats.

The 20th century witnessed a brutal war on this social order and its imperfect decencies. The most destructive part of that war had its first stirrings much earlier, with Rousseau and the German Romantics, who despised the commercial pursuits and private interests of the modern city, seeing them as corrosive of organic community and its moral and symbolic traditions. For such critics, bourgeois virtues were not virtues but corruptions. Even some of the American Founders were not exempt from these anti-urban suspicions. Thomas Jefferson, for instance, extolled farmers as "the chosen people of God if ever He had a chosen people," the rock of republican government, very different from the urban "mobs," who "add just so much to the support of pure government, as sores do to the strength of the human body." (Late in life Jefferson recognized America's need for cities if the nation was to become a great manufacturing power and militarily protect its freedoms—nothing ever got built in the country—and he certainly knew how to enjoy Paris.) By the 19th century "bourgeois" had become, in the words of the Dutch historian Johan Huizinga, "the most pejorative term of all, particularly in the mouths of socialists and artists, and later even of fascists." The bourgeois is the villain of *The Communist Manifesto* and *Das Kapital*. And, as we know from the subsequent "anti-bourgeois" crimes of the communists and Nazis, this fomenting of hatred toward ordinary urban life had dreadful effects.

Leading the anti-bourgeois reaction have been many of the bourgeois themselves. Consider how many Marxists were the sons or daughters of bankers, lawyers, merchants, and others raised in the culture of urbanity: Marx and Engels themselves, then Lenin, Rosa Luxemburg, György Lukács, Herbert Marcuse—and many more, including today's innumerable tenured radicals. Modern bourgeois democracy has a seemingly infinite capacity to produce offspring who detest the social and political regime that has secured their privileges.

François Furet addressed this paradox in his 1999 book, *The Passing of an Illusion: The Idea of Communism in the Twentieth Century*, arguing that communism and fascism exploited two weaknesses in the civilization against which they rebelled. The first is the ideal of equality promised by the "bourgeois city," as Furet dubbed the modern political and economic order. The bourgeois freedoms— to pursue wealth, to strive for happiness, and to forge one's destiny— erode equality. We are not all born with the same propensities and talents, and not all of us have the same luck or the same family circumstances.

Hence, although individual freedom means equal opportunities, it will for that very reason produce unequal outcomes. Communism promised to reach equality in a way that bourgeois society never could. All that was necessary was to crush a few political obstacles and to eradicate the multiplicity of private ends. Contemporary left-liberals such as John Rawls promise something similar, albeit in a less bloodthirsty way. Rawls even raises the prospect of genetic engineering to overcome natural differences, thereby building an egalitarian society on the principles of Huxley's *Brave New World*.

The second fundamental weakness of the bourgeois city, Furet argues, is moral indeterminacy. The liberal political order that has emerged in the West downplays any extra-human dimension, whether natural or supernatural, that might provide firm answers to the ultimate questions of existence. Such existential questions instead become privatized, displaced from the governing sphere to that of culture. This frustrates a natural but, under modern conditions, dangerous impulse in man to see his highest aspirations and deepest meanings completely embodied in the central political authority, as they were, for instance, in the political institutions of Calvin's Geneva.

Furet is keenly aware of the liberations secured by the bourgeois city, its unprecedented freedom from political tyranny, and the dictatorship of poverty. But by contrast with movements that have sought to establish their highest ideals politically, such as communism, fascism, and Nazism, the bourgeois city has seemed to many to be thin, boring, alienating, and cold. Furet's wise book warns the citizens of the West to live with bourgeois imperfections. The alternatives, though perfectionist, are worse than imperfect; they are lethal. And the bourgeois city has never been as alienating, as empty of meaning, as its critics on the left and right have charged. On the contrary, consider Chicago. It is no utopia: it remains crime-plagued; its economy struggles at times; it has a stubbornly entrenched black underclass; and its politics are legendarily corrupt. Yet it is a functioning, living place, filled with the kind of meaningful community—the *gemeinschaftlich* attachments—that anti-urbanists claim the city invariably destroys.

Economist Deirdre McCloskey, returning to Chicago after living in small Iowa City and smaller Granville, Ohio, runs through the Windy City's community scorecard: "30 Episcopal churches within easy driving distance instead of four or five; 70 ethnic groups in bulk instead of two; 20 Irish pubs instead of one." Sure, Chicago has lots of Gesellschaft, or rational, businesslike association, McCloskey adds—but that's because a big city has more of everything. "That's why there are so many people there," she concludes.

The bourgeois city survived its struggle with totalitarianism—just visit post-communist Bratislava, say, or Kraków, and feel the energy on the streets, the bustle of commerce, the sense of possibility that surrounds you. But urban civilization has faced two other enemies whose impact has been ruinous, both in the U.S. and in Europe: the city planners and the liberal establishment. During the post-World War II period, city planners throughout the West fatefully decided to remove their "slums," seeing them as blighted anachronisms in a new rational age. Yet what were slums, argues philosopher Roger Scruton, but the "harmonious classical streets of affordable houses, seeded with local industries, corner shops, schools, and places of worship, that had made it possible for real communities to flourish in the center of our towns"? Poor they might have been, but they were alive and actively reproducing themselves.

In place of the slums came something far worse: the modernist high-rise housing project, surrounded by empty, wind-swept plazas. Right out of the dark imaginings of Le Corbusier and Walter Gropius, the projects immediately became forces for social breakdown and disorder. All public buildings would henceforth be modernist too, lacking facades and jarringly unlike their older architectural neighbors.

Making matters worse, new "rational" zoning regulations now separated what had always gone together: offices would go up in one part of the city, shopping in another, residences in yet another. As Jane Jacobs argued in her classic *The Death and Life of Great American Cities*, these developments robbed neighborhoods of their round-the-clock vitality, in which someone always was at home or at work and could watch the street for signs of trouble or offer a helping hand when needed. Now, zoned for different purposes, whole sections of the city would remain all but uninhabited for parts of the day, save for predators and outlaws. One need only look at ravaged downtown Detroit, throbbing with menace and alienation, to see what the planners and their architect allies helped bring about.

From the 1950s on, as the dark and faceless towers rose up, middle-class families, empowered by the automobile, began fleeing in droves for the suburbs, draining cities of civic and economic vitality. The sprawling suburbanites weren't just fleeing the planners and modernist architects, however, but the 20th century's third anti-urban force—the social policies of the left-liberal establishment. It is hard to overestimate the damage liberals did to the bourgeois city, to urbanity, and thus to the essence of Western civilization itself, beginning in the 1960s. The left-liberals of that decade believed that America (Amerika, as they had it) was a deeply unjust country built on racist attitudes, and that aggressive government action was necessary to lift up the poor and especially poor blacks, who had crowded into cities after World War II; no free market could do the job. As a result of this belief, cities became the breeding ground for a demoralized underclass. Welfare payments undermined self-reliance; passive policing encouraged crime; and schools, given over to Deweyite goals of self-expression and self-esteem, enabled children to leave for the streets, with their ignorance and malice intact.

Not only did these measures fail to help the poor, but they also made cities less and less livable. New York, America's biggest and greatest city, was hardest hit. A liberal-imposed fear of offending minorities, combined with a belief that crime was environmental, so that nothing could really be done about it unless all social problems could be solved first, so hampered law enforcement that whole swathes of the city were left wild zones. Felonies became endemic, scaling to hundreds of thousands a year, with murders hitting a grim high in 1990 of 2,262. Much of the crime was black preying on black, but the whole city suffered. Welfare programs in the city aggressively signed up every poor person in sight, spurred on by academics like Columbia University's Richard Cloward and City University's Frances Fox Piven, who saw the local public-aid system as the cornerstone of urban life and who sought to lay the foundations for a nationwide welfare state. The welfare rolls exceeded one million under liberal Republican mayor John Lindsay in 1972 and reached an all-time high of 1.1 million in 1995, under liberal Democratic mayor David Dinkins. The result, as everyone but the blindest ideologue knows, was a human catastrophe: a culture of permanent government dependency that robbed whole generations of the future. Life on the dole accelerated the breakdown of the black family (some neighborhoods saw illegitimacy rates go past 90 percent)—a result that was further encouraged by the ceaseless liberal campaign to demoralize sexual relations and delegitimize old-fashioned mother-father-children families. Single-parent families, with reduced emotional and financial resources, were more likely to be dependent on welfare, closing the no-exit loop. As Irving Kristol once put it: the "welfare trap" had sprung.

The city's public schools were not going to help anyone escape the trap. Controlled by monolithic and self-interested teachers' unions, their officials propagated failed pedagogies and shrugged as minority students dropped out at alarming rates. New York began spending much more than it could afford, and it drove up taxes to business-killing levels. The city lost most of its Fortune 500 companies, which left for more economically hospitable climes. Movies like *Taxi Driver* and *Escape from New York* started to depict Gotham not as a place where dreams could be made real but as a modern-day Inferno, populated by lost souls and soulless killers. The title of historian Fred Siegel's great book on the urban crisis, *The Future Once Happened Here*, captured the widespread sense that New York had become ungovernable, had exhausted its life force, and would soon expire. Nor did the crisis affect only New York. For a while, it seemed as though the bourgeois city was finished.

Thankfully, that hasn't happened, at least not yet. The 1990s, as Siegel and others have documented, saw a breathtaking rebirth of urbanity. New York led the way out of the urban crisis, just as it had led the way in. Under Mayor Rudy Giuliani and his police commissioner William Bratton, New York said "enough" to high crime.

Cracking down on low-level offenses like aggressive panhandling and prostitution, under the assumption that tolerating such "victimless" crimes encourages more serious criminals to act on their baser impulses, and employing sophisticated computers to map crime while holding police commanders responsible for real crime-reduction results, Bratton's NYPD pulled off the greatest policy success story of the postwar era: a complete turnaround on crime. Felonies plummeted during the Giuliani years and have continued to fall under Mayor Michael Bloomberg, whose top cop, Ray Kelly, has kept in place the older reforms and added some of his own. In fact, serious crimes are down 77 percent, murder included, since the Dinkins-era peak.

Emboldened by the Welfare Reform Act of 1996, which ended the federal entitlement to welfare, Giuliani energetically slashed the welfare rolls, which have also continued to shrink under his successor—down to 345,000 at present, the lowest number since October 1963. Mayor Giuliani also cut some taxes, the first time that had happened in the city for many years (although, alas, Bloomberg has raised taxes since). The lowered crime, slashed welfare rolls, and more friendly business environment enabled the renewal of New York City's economy. People began to talk about how pleasant life in the big city could be. Blacks have benefited perhaps most of all, with once-blighted neighborhoods in Harlem and the Bronx buzzing with investment and growth. Not even the worst day in the city's history, September 11, 2001, could derail the recovery. Even the city planners have become more sensible, at last recognizing the worth of Jacobs-style mixed-use zoning, although the reign of architectural modernism has yet to end, with architects like Frank Gehry and Daniel Libeskind still dominating the competitions. New York's experience shows that the bourgeois city is not fated to extinction. European cities, whose crime rates, other than for murder, are today generally higher than those of U.S. cities, show signs of learning these lessons too. However, the revolution is far from complete, and victories remain precarious.

Middle-class families have started to trickle back into urban areas, but high taxes and unacceptable public schools stand as obstacles to further renewal. The crime turnaround demands perpetual vigilance. And left-wing "community organizers" and interest groups work night and day to bring back the ruinous policies of the liberal era. Worse, they now have their national leader: Barack Obama, a man wedded to a refuted conception of the city and its needs. Conservatives, too often dismissive of cities as left-wing satrapies, need to stand up to this liberal reaction. In so doing, they would be defending the vision of the city that has come down to us from Athens, Jerusalem, Rome, and Genoa. This vision distinguishes Western civilization and provides us with our highest political idea—a society of free citizens, bound together by consent and governed by a law of which they themselves are the authors. Hayek was right: civilization as we know it is inseparable from urban life.

The Limits of Liberty

Roger Scruton

In this concluding essay I bring together some of the principal strands of argument developed by the other authors and suggest the abiding relevance of John Locke's distinction between liberty and license. Individual liberty is a social condition and both cause and effect of a particular kind of social order. License, by contrast, spells the disintegration of society and its fragmentation into a state of nature, as individual appetite becomes sovereign over social responsibility. Many of the things now defended as "liberties" by liberals are in fact forms of license and therefore threats to liberty, while many of the limits to liberty proposed and defended by conservatives are designed to prevent liberty from degenerating into license.

The essays in this book all remind us that liberty remains one of the defining issues of modern politics. It is what is at stake in domestic controversies, in foreign relations, and in the broader ideological movements of our time. The writers have considered the conflict between liberalism and conservatism, the disputes over political correctness in schools and colleges, the emerging issue of religious liberty, the battles over the Constitution, the tension between the European Union and the nation states of Europe, the foreign policy problems created by Russia and China and by the aftermath of communism, and the broader conflict between the West and radical Islam. And in all these matters liberty is a central political value and one of the things most at risk.

In referring to liberty, however, are we referring to a single good or to a multitude of goods? And are there limits to liberty beyond which it ceases to be a good? Such questions are not easy to answer, for in all the areas covered by the writers the controversies and the ambiguities run deep. At the very start of the modern discussions, in his *Essay Concerning Toleration* (1689), John Locke distinguished liberty from license, reminding us that there are freedoms that we abhor and that it is the duty of government to extinguish. Exactly how to identify those "licentious" freedoms remains highly controversial. Moreover, we know that one person's liberty may conflict with another's. Hence libertarians, who believe that the sole aim of government is to protect and amplify the liberty of the citizen, cannot assume that this statement contains the whole of politics. We must still devise the institutions—the minimum or "nightwatchman" state, as Robert Nozick describes it (*Anarchy, State and Utopia*, 1974)—that will reconcile the freedom of each citizen with the freedom of his neighbors while maximizing freedom over all.

But there is a deeper question, about liberty itself. When I unleash my dog, I grant him his liberty to move as he wishes. And we think of this liberty as a good—something an animal needs and enjoys and of which he should not be wrongly deprived. We bewail the fate of pigs raised in narrow cages and unable to turn around for days on end. We believe that animals too need liberty, even if only the liberty to move as their instincts suggest. And without this liberty they suffer.

Yet that is not what we mean by political liberty, which is the freedom of people to pursue their long-term projects without impediment from their fellow citizens or from the state. And it has been argued on many sides that political liberty, in this sense, has been a distinguishing mark of Western civilization, being implicit to our forms of government long before the Enlightenment spelled it out. Brian C. Anderson follows Michael Novak, who, in his 2002 book, *On Two Wings*, rehearses the familiar thesis that Western civilization arose from two powerful spiritual forces, one originating in Athens, the other in Jerusalem, one expressed in Greek political philosophy, the other in "Jewish metaphysics." The Greeks defined liberty as a political condition—the condition of the man who is "owner of himself," as opposed to that of the man who is owned by another. And the ideal *polis* is one that would enable this to be the *normal* condition of citizens within a shared public space. Thus was born the *agora*, the meeting place of the community, in which the whole body of citizens participated in making the laws to which each of them would be subject.

The Jews defined liberty in another way, as an inner condition—the condition of the creature capable of free choices and whose freedom was manifest in his relations with others, in his emotional commitments, and in his sense of accountability before his eternal judge. As Rémi Brague puts the point, "outside the Judeo-Christian tradition, it has been rare for thinkers to suppose that God endowed us with a nature of our own, that freedom is a part of that nature, and that it is through the exercise of freedom, and the errors that inevitably stem from it, that we fulfill God's plan." And he adds that "the mainstream tradition of Islam has certainly regarded freedom, both personal and political, as valuable—but valuable largely as a means to submission."

From the discussions of Anderson and Brague we can conclude that there are two ideas of freedom at issue—freedom as self-ownership, which is the core political idea, and freedom as the capacity for responsible choice, which is the idea that animates the Judaeo-Christian worldview. And, if we follow Brague, the religious tradition that attached us to the second of those ideas supported the political tradition centered on the first. But there is also a tension between the two. The constant attempt to extend the reach of self-ownership raises again the problem that troubled Locke—the problem of distinguishing liberty from license. The point is made in other terms by Judge Bork, in his penetrating discussion of the Constitution: the Supreme Court, in its constant invention of the "rights" necessary to protect the elite lifestyle from legislative control, has also promoted customs and practices that undermine social values and make it far less likely, in the times in which we live, that genuinely free beings, capable of responsible choices, will emerge.

Social thinkers like Charles Murray and James Q. Wilson have documented the domestic and sexual anarchy that surrounds so many children from birth and the damage that it inflicts on their development into responsible adults. It is surely evident that this anarchy could be limited only by a legislature determined to reinforce family values with whatever sanctions and incentives are available to it—for instance, by restricting the availability of pornography, by offering incentives for traditional marriage and withholding endorsement from other kinds of sexual union, by ceasing to reward feckless behavior through the welfare system and by penalizing fathers who abandon their children. But all such policies involve taking sides in what should be, according to the liberal orthodoxy, matters of individual moral choice. As the Supreme Court expressed the point in the celebrated case of *Planned Parenthood v. Casey*, "At the heart of liberty is the right to define one's own concept of existence, of meaning, of the universe, and the mystery of human life." Any attempt by the legislature to forbid activities that this or that liberal conscience might seize upon as essential to the goal of self-fulfillment or as justified by "the mystery of human life" can be struck down as unconstitutional. And the effect of this over the last 40 years has been to erode the distinction between liberty and license to the point where the legislative privileges once offered to marriage and the family have now entirely disappeared.

Locke believed that license involves extending liberties beyond the point at which one person's liberties can be reconciled with the liberties of others. And this can be witnessed today, as Judge Bork's examples show. The rights protected by the Supreme Court grant freedoms to parents while removing them from their children. Children in the womb don't have the right to life, and if they are born nevertheless, they certainly have no right to parental protection or to the normal comforts of family life. And this suggests a deep point at issue between liberals and conservatives in the constitutional battles of our time, the one claiming space for adults to enjoy their brief time in the sun, the other hoping to constrain adult behavior in the interests of future generations. Freedom that can be enjoyed by one generation only by condemning the next to dependency surely deserves the name of license.

An interesting twist is added to this argument by Robert P. George, who shows the extent to which liberals on the American campus are prepared to intimidate students who fail to endorse their orthodoxies regarding sex. An interesting paradox has begun to emerge. Conservative defenders of liberty against license are being deprived of their liberties—and in particular liberty of speech and opinion—by the defenders of license. In the new campus censorship we begin to see the depth of the conflict here. The old idea of a liberal education emphasized the value of education in freeing the mind and inducing habits of informed and responsible choice. Education was seen as a means to liberty in its inward meaning, the meaning that Anderson and Brague associate with the original Jewish revelation. Now, however, the goal of education is often seen as a more outward liberty, associated with an ever-expanding sphere of individual rights, and a breaking free from the constraints of traditional morality in the interests of self-expression. To conservative opinion, this involves the pursuit of license. To liberal opinion, it involves the pursuit of liberty in its only objective form.

As I suggested, the conflicts and ambiguities here run deep. We all of us value the liberties associated with the Greek ideal of self-ownership, and we are all aware that liberty must be restricted, if only to ensure that the liberty of each person is compatible with the liberty of everyone else. The question is where to draw the line and on what principle? There is a schematic answer to that question, which holds that individuals should be granted those liberties necessary to ensure that they have effective *sovereignty* over their own lives. And this is an answer on which liberals and conservatives may in principle agree. If there is any feature of Western political systems that distinguishes them from their rivals in the modern world it is this—that they are designed not just to govern people, but also to guarantee their sovereignty. Individuals in Western states are sovereign over their own households; they enjoy consumer sovereignty through the market and political sovereignty through elections. They are sovereign in their projects and careers, in that neither the state nor their fellow citizens can compel them in a favored direction. They have a right to life, limb, and property, and these rights are secure against the state, subject to principles of good behavior enshrined in the criminal law, and recognized by all, or almost all, as valid. Of course, liberals and conservatives will differ as to how far these individual rights should extend and the ways in which sovereignty can be properly exercised. But they differ only because they are both pursuing the same idea—the idea of a society of self-owning individuals, each of whose sovereignty is compatible with an equal sovereignty granted to everyone else.

Seeing things that way, we will surely agree with Paul Johnson's recognition of private property as a cornerstone of liberty. A property right is a fragment of individual sovereignty: it says that the use, exploitation, or consumption of a certain thing can take place only with the consent of the individual owner, whose interest will be protected by the law. As Johnson points out, private ownership of land was one of the factors that forced the kings of England to grant liberties to their subjects. And it is the lack of private ownership that left the victims of communism unprotected against the communist party and its members. Likewise, the invasion of property rights by the unscrupulous use of "eminent domain" is a growing threat to liberty in America. Private property enables us to close a door on our oppressors and open it to our friends. It enables us to deal freely in goods and strike bargains for our needs. The free market is a natural extension of private property, and as we have seen in the dire history of 20th-century Europe, the abolition of the market economy went everywhere hand in hand with the oppression of the individual and his subjection to the state.

As Anne Applebaum argues, however, the free market is only one part of social liberty. Her telling comparison of Poland and Russia since the communist collapse shows that private property and the market are not enough to establish the kind of freedom that we in the West take for granted. Equally important, and perhaps more important when it comes to human ideals and social fulfilment, is the liberty of association. For this is what permits civil society to grow outside the control of the state. Under communism people were permitted to form families. But any other form of association was regarded with suspicion, and almost all private societies were outlawed. It was not only schools, universities, and medical facilities that were monopolized by the state. Every little platoon, from the symphony orchestra to the local brass band, from the scout movement to the philately club, was either controlled by the party or outlawed. Even the churches came under communist party supervision—except in Poland, where, as Applebaum shows, they created a unique space in which civil society endured through the years of darkness. Hence it was in Poland that the overthrow of communism began.

Freedom of association is so evidently a part of individual sovereignty that you would assume that both conservatives and liberals endorse it. But this is not so, and for a very interesting reason. Associations make distinctions; they breed hierarchies; they foster competition; they are sources of local pride and individual aspiration. In other words, they are, potentially at least, the enemies of equality. Hence they are apt to fall under liberal suspicion. Private schools, for example, have been heavily penalized in Europe, by those who believe them (rightly) to be the source of social inequalities. Private clubs that exclude women have been outlawed in America, and associations like the Boy Scouts, which (for understandable reasons) refuse to employ homosexuals, have been subjected to discriminatory treatment—most notably by the City Council of Philadelphia, which has forced the Scouts to leave the property that the organization once gave to the city.

The communist move to control all associations, to outlaw charitable trusts and to make every social institution into a "transmission belt," was simply the extreme example of a motive that remains widespread in modern societies—the desire to neutralize those exercises of human freedom that offend some code of equality, "inclusion," or political correctness. As a result, freedoms our grandparents took for granted—the freedom, for example, to employ whom you want in your business, to admit whom you want to your school or university, to fire someone who is in breach of his contract, even to offer your services as your conscience dictates—have now been limited or even confiscated by the state. In a recent case, a Californian couple who ran a photography business were found guilty under anti-discrimination laws when they declined the request to photograph (for a fee) a lesbian "wedding," on the grounds that it was not consonant with their Christian principles to be present at such an event, still less to endorse it with their services. Here is another telling example of liberty confiscated by the advocates of what many would regard as license.

In America the hostility to free association on behalf of "inclusion" has been most vividly apparent in the feminist movement. But, as Christina Sommers points out, feminists have airbrushed from the history of their movement the true advocates of liberty in order to idolize the radicals who were more interested in conscripting women than in granting them their freedom. The conservative feminists, whom Sommers credits with the *real* work of emancipating women in the 19th century, were far more influential than the radical feminists who are currently identified as the movement's founders. But they were traditionalist and family-centered. As Sommers puts it, they "embraced rather than rejected women's established roles as homemakers, caregivers, and providers of domestic tranquillity—and [they] promoted women's rights by redefining, strengthening, and expanding those roles. Conservative feminists argued that a practical, responsible femininity could be a force for good in the world beyond the family, through charitable works and more enlightened politics and government." In short, the conservative feminists, such as Frances Willard, adhered to the traditional image of woman as "the angel in the house." They did not wish to destroy the family or the man's place within it but to grant self-ownership to the wife and mother on whom the peace of the household depends. Such feminists were liberals, not in the modern sense of demanding state-enforced equality but in the classical sense, of demanding rights of self-ownership that would give women the same sovereignty over their lives as that enjoyed by men.

As Sommers points out, the home of radical feminism is not the family or the workplace; it is the campus. Radical feminism is an opinionated movement, dependent on the massive rents on middle-class incomes that are available to those who can control the university curriculum. The campus feminists show all the intolerance documented by George in his review of academic freedom. They are notorious for devising courses that impose ideological tests for entrance and successful exit, that ignore all countervailing arguments and alternative visions, and that have the closing of the student mind as their implicit goal. And they have more or less wrecked the traditional curriculum in the humanities, by inventing the specious subject of "women's studies" and by promoting "feminist readings" of classical texts—in other words, readings that undermine the authority of those texts and show that we should not in fact be reading them. Moreover, by advocating suspicion and hostility to men, the campus feminists have begun to recruit young women to a way of life that condemns as an institutionalized path to oppression the most important liberty that a woman can enjoy—the liberty to be a wife and mother, in a family home. For Simone de Beauvoir, indeed, that is a liberty no woman should be granted.

Nevertheless, liberty of opinion still exists in Western societies, and although I have done my academic career no good by writing the above paragraph, Encounter Books will not suffer from publishing it. To what do we owe this great achievement? The test case, as Seamus Hasson shows, is religion. Religious opinions are unlike scientific opinions or even political opinions, in that they are expressions of existential commitment. Religious believers identify their deepest interests, their community, their sense of life's purpose, through their faith, and react to those who question it with suspicion and distrust, if not downright hostility. How then can a society be constituted so as to permit the peaceful coexistence of rival religions, and to protect people who live by one faith from the intolerance of those who live by another? As Hasson argues, the American Founders took the bold step of addressing this problem in the Constitution, introducing the "no establishment" clause in order to ensure that the state would remain neutral in religious disputes, standing above them and maintaining in the face of them the equal right of every citizen to the opinions that are his.

As Hasson reminds us, the purpose was not to repress religion or to exclude it from the affairs of state. On the contrary, the purpose was to *permit* religion, and to allow people of faith the right to practice and express their beliefs without hindrance from those who do not share them and without hindrance from the state. Once again, however, the defender of liberty comes up against the advocate of license. Religion is one of the most important vehicles for the passing on of social order, moral values, and spiritual capital. Religious people are by nature hostile to license, strive to control their sexual lives, and are usually first in the exercise of those conservative virtues that get up the liberal nose. They are eager to teach children the norms of restraint and decency; they are in favor of discipline and respect and on the whole support the adult against the adolescent in all matters where the two conflict. Hence the advocates of self-expression and moral anarchy would like to marginalize religious people and remove their influence from the public space of our culture. To this end they have reinterpreted the "no establish-ment" clause not as *permitting* religion but as *forbidding* it. Religion, they argue, is excluded from every office, activity, or social arena gov-erned (however indirectly) by the state—so there cannot be prayers or Bible classes in public schools, there cannot be any acknowledg-ment of God, the Ten Commandments, or the ascendancy of the Christian religion in any legal or political institution, and those who receive state support for their charitable work among the poor and the broken-hearted cannot use the Bible as their guide. Never has a more effective means been discovered of cutting off a whole people from its inheritance of moral and spiritual capital than this one, whereby the Constitution devised to permit religious beliefs is used as an instrument for suppressing them.

This returns me to Rémi Brague's discussion of the Judaeo-Christian inheritance. As Brague points out, the Judaeo-Christian tradition has portrayed God as standing in a free relation to his creatures. He has not sought to compel our love—for love is not love when forced. He has sought to reach an agreement, a covenant, which will govern not only our relations with Him but also our rela-tions with one another. That seems to imply a contrast with the Islamic vision. *Islam* means submission, and although this submis-sion should be freely undertaken, it cannot be freely escaped. Hence it is easy to interpret the Quran as forbidding us to question, or even to interpret, the direct commands of God. Those who cite the holy book in justification of oppressive customs, such as forced marriage, female circumcision, the stoning of adulterers, and the sequestra-tion of women do so with no sense of blasphemy. They may have mistaken the letter of the text, but they are confident in its spirit. In their eyes, the God of the Quran is an angry old man with a beard, a kind of super-mullah, as fierce and humorless as his spokesmen here below.

That this is a travesty of Islam goes without saying. But it is a travesty with a large and popular following, rooted in a long-standing way of reading the Quranic verses. And it contrasts with a central strand of the Christian tradition, to which we owe what is perhaps the most important guarantee of liberty in the modern world, the rise of a secular jurisdiction. The privatization of religious law was clearly a part of Jesus's mission, and one of the reasons he aroused such hostility from the Jewish religious authorities. His striking pronouncement in the story of the tribute money, that we should render unto Caesar what is Caesar's and unto God what is God's, has served as authority down the centuries for the view that, in public matters, it is human and not divine government that should be obeyed. This idea gained credibility through St. Paul's letters, influenced as they were by Roman law and by the knowledge that the early Church enjoyed the protection of a developed system of secular law. This law did not claim religious authority and was tolerant of all gods who did not openly confront it with intransigent demands. Even if religious edicts crept back into European jurisdictions after the triumph of Christianity, the Roman vision of sovereignty as exercised through secular law survived into modern times. It served as the foundation of national (in other words territorial) jurisdictions and shaped legal systems in which religious diversity is not merely permitted but openly tolerated, as being no concern of the secular state.

This kind of secular jurisdiction has found its home in the nation state, and—as Jeremy Rabkin points out—the nation state has been the greatest guarantor of freedom in the modern world, precisely because it establishes a territorial, rather than a religious, jurisdiction. Such a jurisdiction enables the nation state to treat citizenship, rather than creed, as the criterion of membership and enables it to adjudicate conflicts between people of different faiths.

Once again, however, we find a growing conflict between conservative and liberal over the role of the nation state and its claims to allegiance. Conservatives have, on the whole, accepted nationality as a sphere of local duties and loyalties, defining an inheritance and a community that has a right to pass on its values from generation to generation. The nation may indeed be the best that we now have, by way of a society linking the dead to the unborn, in the manner extolled by Burke. And for this very reason it arouses the hostility of liberals, who are constantly searching for a place outside loyalty and obedience, from which all human claims can be judged. Hence, in the conflicts of our times, while conservatives leap to the defense of the nation and its interests, wishing to maintain its integrity and to enforce its law, liberals advocate trans-national initiatives, inter-national courts, and doctrines of universal rights, all of which, they believe, should stand in judgment over the nation and hold it to account.

Out of this conflict has arisen yet another conflict between liberty and license. The liberal position tends to found itself on the idea of human rights and to espouse universal jurisdiction, as upholding human rights against the governments of nation states. Conservatives, witnessing the behavior of the U.S. Supreme Court, have become suspicious of the "rights" idea. When something is a fundamental right under the Constitution, then it becomes an abso-lute claim in the hands of the individual, and one that cannot be limited or compromised by public interest. It needs only one person successfully to argue that some particular piece of pornography falls under the protected category of free speech for the entire mass of offensive material to be thenceforth protected absolutely, lifted above the world of legal and political compromise, and given a pro-tection that no normal and worthy human interest could ever hope for. Hence "rights" talk is as useful in the cause of license as it is in the cause of liberty.

Rights, as the liberal American jurist Ronald Dworkin puts it (*Taking Rights Seriously*, 1977), are trumps. If my interest is some-thing I want, while yours is something you have a right to, then, in any conflict, it is you whom the law will protect, not me, even if my interest is more fundamental to my well-being than yours is to your well-being, and even if a compromise solution would be for the common good. Rights are rescued from the political process and become non-negotiable possessions of those who can claim them. They give the courts precedence over the legislature and allow unelected judges to undo the most elaborately thought-through and profoundly needed legislation in order to protect the interests of the individual, however unimportant his interests might be. Rights therefore constitute a serious danger to the political process, as well as an absolute necessity if that process is to be founded in consent. Hence we should be meticulous in defining them and show a true awareness of what is at stake. This awareness, needless to say, is vanishing from the political culture of our age, as more and more people scramble to define as rights those interests they wish to safeguard forever from invasion.

This is particularly so when it comes to international courts, which do not have to bear the cost of their decisions and don't have to reconcile the rights they grant with the many interests that conflict with them. Hence international courts provide a perfect forum for people who wish to advance their own interests without concern for the conflicting interests of others. Here is a simple example: the careful attempt to reconcile conflicting interests on an overcrowded island has led the English Parliament to pass complex and sensitive planning laws that control building in the countryside, and forbid people to reside where they choose. But the European Court of Human Rights has determined that ethnic "travelers" (i.e., gypsies) have a right to their "traditional life style," which involves putting their trailers wherever they settle. This right trumps the interests of English residents, even when the travelers are not British citizens. The result has been massive conflict in the English countryside, leading to murder and arson. In a similar way international courts have defended the "rights" of terrorists against the laws designed to suppress them and the "rights" of migrants against laws that limit their conditions of entry.

Look at the growing list of rights defined and upheld by the U.N. and the various international bodies, and you will see the way in which agendas have taken over from liberties in defining the rights of the individual. The U.N. Human Rights Council is currently policing the world for signs of "Islamophobia," supposedly an offense against human rights of which the U.S. and its allies are principally guilty. The European Court of Human Rights has defined "non-discrimination" as a human right, obliging the European Commission to incorporate this condition as a limitation on EU legislation. One result of this has been to compel national parliaments to close down institutions that discriminate on grounds of "sexual orientation," so that Catholic adoption agencies can no longer function within the law. As the two examples show, the liberal agenda is no more likely to be advanced by trans-national law than the opposite agenda of the Islamists, but in both cases the principal casualty is liberty.

Where does this leave the advocate of liberty in the world today? Looking back over our series of essays, we can perhaps draw a few tentative conclusions. First, we must recognize that liberty is not the same as equality, and that those who call themselves liberals are far more interested in equalizing than in liberating their fellows. Second, the pursuit of liberty often disguises a hostility to established moral norms. When Adam Smith made freedom central to his vision of the modern economy, he was clear that freedom and morality are two sides of a coin. A free society is a community of free beings, bound by the laws of sympathy and by the obligations of family love. It is not a society of people released from all moral constraint, for that is precisely the opposite of a society. Without moral constraint there can be no cooperation, no family commitment, no long-term prospects, no hope of economic, let alone social, order. And, interestingly, as we have seen, the advocates of equality and the advocates of license tend to be one and the same. Morality, they believe, is none of our business; the state is in charge.

Finally we should recognize that this habit of calling upon the state, to take charge of matters that were once the concern of individual initiative and private charity, is the surest sign that the inner liberty shown in responsible choice is disappearing from our society. Its disappearance is both the cause of liberal policies and the natural effect of them. People are less and less inclined to take responsibility for their lives, to commit themselves to others or to social networks, to engage in charitable work or to solve by free initiative what they can summon the state to take charge of instead. And by invoking the state in this way they prepare the way for a loss of political liberty. The state comes with an agenda: it is less interested in freeing people than in equalizing them, less interested in upholding responsible choice than in extending its relief to the irresponsible. In the growth and the operation of the modern state, therefore, we see the way in which the two kinds of liberty—self-ownership and responsible choice—grow and decline together. And we see what the cause of the true conservative must be—liberty, in both senses of the word.

Notes on Contributors

Kevin J. "Seamus" Hasson is founder, chairman of the board, and president of the Becket Fund for Religious Liberty. He is also the author of *The Right to Be Wrong: Ending the Culture War Over Religion in America*.

Paul Johnson is the author of many books, including *A History of the English People*, *Modern Times*, and *A History of the American People*.

Anne Applebaum is a columnist for the *Washington Post*. Her book *Gulag: A History*, won the 2004 Pulitzer Prize for nonfiction. She lives in Poland.

Rémi Brague is a professor of philosophy at the Sorbonne and at the University of Munich. His books include *The Law of God* and *The Wisdom of the World: The Human Experience of the Universe in Western Thought*.

Robert H. Bork is a distinguished fellow at the Hudson Institute. His books include *Slouching Towards Gomorrah: Modern Liberalism and American Decline* (1996; reissued 2003) and *Coercing Virtue: The Worldwide Rule of Judges* (2003).

Robert P. George is McCormick Professor of Jurisprudence at Princeton University and director of its James Madison Program in

American Ideals and Institutions. He is the author of many books, including *Natural Law, Liberalism and Morality* (2001) and *Embryo: A Defense of Human Life* (2008).

Christina Hoff Sommers is a resident scholar at the American Enterprise Institute and the author of *Who Stole Feminism? How Women Have Betrayed Women* (1995) and *The War Against Boys: How Misguided Feminism Is Harming Young Men* (2001).

Jeremy Rabkin is professor of law at George Mason University School of Law and the author of *Law Without Nations?*, *The Case for Sovereignty*, and *Why Sovereignty Matters*.

Brian C. Anderson is the editor of *City Journal* and the author of *A Manifesto for Media Freedom* (with Adam Theirer), *Democratic Capitalism and Its Discontents*, and *South Park Conservatives*, among other works. He writes often for the *Wall Street Journal*, the *Los Angeles Times*, and many other publications.

Roger Scruton is a resident scholar at the American Enterprise Institute and author most recently of *Culture Counts* and *Beauty, A Short Introduction*.

Index

end/20